Praise for *12 Truths & a Lie*

"There are some common questions that most of us have asked, or likely will ask at some point in life. We may not always be able to find the words or the courage to ask them out loud, but at the very least, these are the questions our hearts have wrestled with. In *Twelve Truths and a Lie*, my friend and fellow pastor J.D. Greear gives refreshingly honest answers to your most poignant questions. Whether you're the one asking the questions or you know someone who is, this book will be a great resource."

—Kyle Idleman, senior pastor of Southeast Christian Church, and bestselling author of *When Your Way Isn't Working*

"Common questions for us all: If God is really in control, why is there so much suffering? If I'm really a Christian, why do I keep on sinning? When Paul said, 'No temptation has overtaken you that is not common to man,' you can basically apply that to questions too. Some of us are too afraid to ask our questions out loud. In *Twelve Truths and a Lie*, J.D. Greear not only asks the questions—he answers them. Part insight, part illustration, and totally honest; read to find the Biblical truth."

—Mark Moore, teaching pastor of Christ Church of the Valley, and bestselling author of *CORE 52*

12 TRUTHS
& A LIE

12 TRUTHS & A LIE

Answers to Life's Biggest Questions

J.D. GREEAR

with Troy Schmidt

BOOKS

FRANKLIN, TENNESSEE

K-LOVE BOOKS

5700 West Oaks Blvd.
Rocklin, CA 95765

Published by K-LOVE Books, an imprint of EMF Publishing, LLC, 5700 West Oaks Blvd., Rocklin, CA 95765.

Unless otherwise noted, scripture quotations are from the ESV® Bible (The Holy Bible, English Standard Version®), copyright © 2001 by Crossway, a publishing ministry of Good News Publishers. Used by permission. All rights reserved.

Scripture quotations marked CSB are from the Christian Standard Bible.® Copyright © 2017 by Holman Bible Publishers. Used by permission. Christian Standard Bible® and CSB® are federally registered trademarks of Holman Bible Publishers.

Scripture quotations marked KJV are from the King James Version. Public domain.

Scripture quotations marked NIV are from the Holy Bible, New International Version,® NIV.® Copyright © 1973, 1978, 1984, 2011 by Biblica, Inc.® Used by permission of Zondervan. All rights reserved worldwide. www.zondervan.com. The "NIV" and "New International Version" are trademarks registered in the United States Patent and Trademark Office by Biblica, Inc.®

Scripture quotations marked NKJV are from the New King James Version.® Copyright © 1982 by Thomas Nelson. Used by permission. All rights reserved.

The majority of deity pronouns in this book are lowercase according to the Chicago Manual of Style.

Printed in the United States of America.

First edition: 2023
10 9 8 7 6 5 4 3 2 1

ISBN: 978-1-954201-51-4 (Hardcover)
ISBN: 978-1-954201-52-1 (E-book)
ISBN: 978-1-954201-53-8 (Audiobook)

Publisher's Cataloging-in-Publication data

Names: Greear, J. D., 1973, author. | Schmidt, Troy, author.
Title: 12 truths and a lie: answers to lifes biggest questions / J.D. Greear; with Troy Schmidt.
Description: Includes bibliographical references. | Franklin, TN: K-LOVE Books, 2023.
Identifiers: ISBN: 978-1-954201-51-4 (hardcover) | 978-1-954201-52-1 (e-book) | 978-1-954201-53-8 (audio)
Subjects: LCSH Christian life. | Conduct of life. |
BISAC RELIGION / Christian Living / Spiritual Growth |
RELIGION / Faith | RELIGION / Christian Living / Inspirational
Classification: LCC BV4501.2. G74 2023 | DDC 241--dc23

Cover design by Gearbox, David Carlson
Interior design by PerfecType, Nashville, TN

To Chad Price, Matt Miglarese, and Cliff Johnson
who help me trust in the God who
"calls into existence the things that do not (yet) exist."
We're just getting started.
And to all of our faithful "Ask Me Anything"
listeners and to the people of The Summit Church,
whose questions inspired and shaped this book.

CONTENTS

INTRODUCTION

The Lie

(That Keeps You from the Truths)

As a pastor, I get asked a lot of questions.

So many, in fact, that I created a podcast called *Ask Me Anything* that's been listened to almost two million times. Our listeners submit some pretty good sticklers. Some of the best ones include:

- What color is God?
- Won't heaven get boring after a while?
- Does God care if Duke wins their next game?
- Is reading Harry Potter books wrong?
- Do I have to close my eyes to pray?
- Can I play the lottery if I promise to give the church 10 percent?

I also pastor The Summit Church in North Carolina, which has a congregation of twelve thousand people and fifteen campuses in the Research Triangle, consistently rated one of the most educated places in the country.[1] You don't think I get some zingers from them too?

I used to get nervous when people reached out with questions. I'd think, *What if they ask me something I don't know?* And sure, there's plenty I don't know. But over time, I've come to realize that most people generally ponder the same questions. I still get asked questions *all the time*, but they are rarely novel or surprising. Most questions center on the same issues. They may not be easy issues. But they're incredibly common.

That's the purpose of this book: to share with you the questions I hear most often—and the truths that flow from them. While these aren't the *only* conundrums I'm asked, they rank in the top twelve. My guess is that some of your most pressing questions are in here too.

I also decided to include *one lie* in this book of twelve truths.

---

1. Adam McCann, "2023's Most & Least Educated Cities in America," WalletHub, July 17, 2023, https://wallethub.com/edu/e/most-and-least-educated-cities/6656. According to WalletHub, we have two of the top ten most educated cities in America: Durham and Raleigh. "Top 101 cities with the most people having Master's or Doctorate degrees (population 50,000+)," City-Data, accessed August 4, 2023, https://www.city-data.com/top2/h182.html. Not to be outdone, Chapel Hill—the third member of the Research Triangle—actually outpaces both Raleigh and Durham in terms of per capita population with advanced degrees, at a whopping 37 percent.

You know the game Two Truths and a Lie, right? You tell people two true bizarre-ish things about yourself and one lie. Everyone has to guess which is the lie. (For an extrovert like me, the game is a ton of fun. For introverts, it's a nightmare.) Let's do a round right now. Which one is the lie?

1. Davy Crockett was my great, great, great, great uncle.
2. I once shared avocado toast with Nicolas Cage.
3. In high school, I placed fourth in the state spelling bee.

Which ones do you think are true, and which is the lie? You'll have to wait until the final chapter to find out.

For those who couldn't wait and just skimmed the last chapter to find out, welcome back. I think we have some stuff coming up in this book about patience that will be particularly relevant for you.

Back to our main point: Rather than only offering twelve truths, I decided to mix it up by including one lie as well.

Unlike the game, however, I'm not going to keep you in total suspense about the lie. In fact, the entire point of having a lie is to clarify what's *true*. This lie has wreaked havoc in the hearts of many believers, and it's time to call out the lie for what it is.

What is the lie? I'll introduce it now, but you'll have to wait until the closing chapter for the final answer to it. Here you go:

The lie: If you have doubts and difficult questions, you're a bad Christian, or maybe not a Christian at all.

In my two decades of being a pastor, I've learned that many people never voice their questions for fear that the question, or doubt, reveals some deeply problematic element of their faith. Real Christians, they assume, never have these questions. Christianity comes naturally for them.

I used to think like that. And when I finally got the courage to start asking some of my questions, I found that a lot of other people, some of whom had grown up in church, had the same ones but were afraid to ask. People in our congregation seem to connect with me *the most* when I verbalize a question I've always had about Christianity— and then attempt to answer it.

It's okay to have questions. It's actually good and healthy. Jesus's disciples certainly did.

In a thought often attributed to nineteenth-century British pastor Charles Spurgeon, doubt is a foot poised to go forward or backward in your faith. If you're honest with your doubts and seek the truth, I believe you'll find your faith deepened, your mind enlightened, and your life enriched— all through a greater intimacy with God.

My prayer for you is that you will enter this book with a desire to be drawn closer to God in the process. Here's my promise to you: I will answer each question according to what God's Word says—the truth! You don't need J. D. Greear's opinions or insights on these things. You need to know what's true. So I've done everything I can to remove myself and my preferences from the answers—especially if the question has to do with Duke. (While we're on the topic, God doesn't hate Duke. They did choose his archenemy, the devil, as their mascot, but I'm sure he finds a way to love them anyway.)

I hope this book finds its way to people checking out this faith-in-Jesus thing, to those who are new to the Christian life, and also to experienced Christians who are looking for ways to better answer similar questions when they're asked at school, church, or work.

If you have more questions, I would love to hear them. Email your questions to requests@jdgreear.com. We might even devote an *Ask Me Anything* podcast to it!

J. D. Greear
May 2023

How Can I Know for Sure I'll Go to Heaven?

The other day I made a decision to sit in a chair. I walked into a room and saw the chair I wanted to sit in. I stood before it and said, "Oh great and mighty chair of chairs, thou art the goodest of chairs in all the universe. Whereforeas now I wish to sit in thy glory, completely surrendering myself to thee. I ask thee to be my personal chair. In the name of the manufacturer, the distributor, and the sales force, amen."

Then I sat in the chair, and my life has never ever been the same.

Before you call the doctors, for real I have never asked a chair into my heart. I also have never approached a chair, flipped it over, tested the legs, researched the manufacturer, called the builders, checked reviews, quizzed a focus group, or asked around the office about what they thought of the chair before I sat in it.

Every day I put my faith in dozens of chairs. Some I'm very familiar with and some are absolute strangers to me.

I've used this example in church, even bringing people onstage to place their trust formally and officially in "The Chair," and nobody has ever asked questions or examined the chair before sitting down. When I ask them to sit, they sit, having complete and total faith to surrender their life into that chair.

But think about it—it's kind of risky. If that chair has a bad leg, the person could fall backward and either hurt or humiliate themselves. Or if a trapdoor was under the chair, a pit of alligators could be waiting for them. Or maybe it's armed with an ejection mechanism and—*boom!*—through the ceiling and four hundred feet into the air they will go like Wile E. Coyote.

I've gone too far, so let me make my point: Relaxing onto a chair has some important similarities to becoming a Christian.

One of the questions I have been asked repeatedly throughout the years is: How can I know that I am a Christian? For that matter, what *is* a Christian, exactly?

Some people assume you can't know and that God wants to keep you guessing. That way, they believe, you won't take your salvation for granted. Instead, you'll keep working at it, going to church, being nice, and paying all your parking fines—as if heaven is the ultimate carrot and hell is the ultimate stick.

Jesus, however, thought differently. He said, "And this is the will of him who sent me, that I should lose nothing of all that he has given me" (John 6:39).

Jesus sounded certain of who is on his side and who he will take to heaven. The trouble is, we often don't. But I have yet to meet a Christian who doesn't want to know, *for certain*, that they're saved.

Stop Asking Jesus Into Your Heart

I wrote a book in 2013 called *Stop Asking Jesus Into Your Heart*. In it, I explained that if *The Guinness Book of World Records* had a record for the number of times someone had prayed the sinner's prayer, I'm pretty sure I would hold it.

By the time I left for college, I had probably prayed the sinner's prayer no fewer than five thousand times. You think I'm joking. I'm not. Every time a speaker gave an invitation to be saved, I'd take it. I've been saved in youth camps all over the nation, at least once in every denomination. I got baptized four times. It got pretty embarrassing. The church gave me my own locker in the backstage changing room—just in case. (That last one *is* a joke . . . but only barely.)

I just wanted to know. I desperately wanted to be sure I was a Christian. Salvation is not the kind of thing someone wants to be wrong about. I shivered in fear over the thought of standing in the heavenly check-in line while Peter (who, in popular lore, has been reduced to a heavenly concierge) says, "I don't see your reservation with us. What's your name again?" I could respond by saying, "Let me talk to your manager," but that likely won't get me anywhere. And by then it will be too late.

I first prayed a prayer when I was five, but then one day in Sunday school, my teacher read this passage in Matthew where Jesus was speaking to a group of really religious people.

> Not everyone who says to me, "Lord, Lord," will enter the kingdom of heaven, but the one who does the will of my Father who is in heaven. On that day many will say to me, "Lord, Lord, did we not prophesy in your name, and cast out demons in your name, and do many mighty works in your name?" And then will I declare to them, "I never knew you; depart from me, you workers of lawlessness." (Matthew 7:21–23)

That was when the doubting started. I wondered, *Am I part of the crowd Jesus doesn't know and will one day say to them, "Get out of my face"*? I mean, the people in Jesus's list are not too shabby. They prophesied (preached)! They cast out demons! I don't know about your church, but when you get assigned to be on the demon-exorcism squad at our church, you're on varsity.

A recent Barna study showed that while 68 percent of Americans identify as Christian, two-thirds of that group have literally no regular presence in any kind of church, nor even a semblance of practice of the Christian faith. Many of them prayed the sinner's prayer. But neither their lifestyles nor their worldviews are distinguishable from those of their non-Christian neighbors.[2]

Now, when these people hear that they need Jesus to be saved, they think, *Oh . . . been there, done that. . . . I've prayed the prayer, filled out the card. I'm good. Even my grandma saw me do it. It was super meaningful. Her tearstains are still on the page.*

Most likely, the people in the Matthew 7 group have similar qualities:

- They prayed the sinner's prayer.
- They read the Bible.
- They were active in their churches: they went on mission trips, memorized verses, or volunteered in the kids' ministry.
- They felt bad about their mistakes and considered themselves moral people.

What Matthew 7 told me is that having prayed a prayer, being involved in church, feeling guilt, and memorizing the Bible won't do you a lick of good in that final moment.

Maybe you're saying, "Wait. I thought the Bible said that if you want to be saved, you just 'call on the name of the Lord' and ask Jesus into your heart" (Romans 10:13;

2. "Signs of Decline & Hope Among Key Metrics of Faith," Barna Group, March 4, 2020, https://www.barna.com/research/changing-state-of-the-church/.

Revelation 3:20). Yes, but that passage isn't talking about praying a magical prayer. It is supposed to be an expression of repentance and faith in the gospel, which is not a quick-prayer thing, but a whole-life-reorientation thing.

By the way, I had a good time trying to explain the title of *Stop Asking Jesus Into Your Heart* to my nine-year-old daughter, Kharis. When I told her the title, she said, "Dad, why would you ever want to tell somebody not to do that?"

After I explained what I was trying to tell people—that it's not the prayer that saves but the faith in Jesus that does—she responded, "Well, that doesn't sound like a very long book. . . . How long is it?"

"About 120 pages," I said.

"Oh, Dad, that's too long. You could say that in about ten pages." She was right. And that's what this chapter is.

So that's the question: What, exactly, is saving faith, and how can we know for sure we have it? Because it seems a lot of people who *should* have assurance don't, and a lot of others *have* assurance . . . but shouldn't.

Let's talk about true salvation in Jesus Christ, and I'll try to do it in about ten pages. Here you go, Kharis.

Give Me Some Credit

The real questions here are: Who belongs to God? Who does Jesus consider his followers? And who will go to heaven? In other words, *who are the true Christians?*

This always leads me to the cliché question made popular by evangelist Billy Graham that went like this: "If you were to die tonight and stand before God, and if he were to ask, 'Why should I let you into heaven?'—what would you say?" (For some reason, people only ever died at night in those days.)

Here's what Scripture says: "To the one who does not work but believes in him who justifies the ungodly, his faith is counted as righteousness" (Romans 4:5).

I had a seminary professor who said this was the most important verse in the New Testament. You may have other verses you consider to be your favorite, but Romans 4:5 is certainly the clearest explanation of what makes someone God's child.

Becoming a child of God means understanding that you can do literally nothing yourself to be right with God and then believing that God *has already done* everything necessary to make you right with him, just as he said he did. These two things—the recognition that *you couldn't* and the belief that *God did like he said*—define the faith that is counted as righteousness.

Let's focus on that word *counted*. It comes from a very important Greek word, *logizomai*, which was used in accounting procedures. *Logizomai* meant that some value had been added to your account. If I owed a debt to the bank, whenever I paid back a portion of what I owed, that much would be credited, or *logizomai'ed*, to my account.

Paul is saying that when God sees your trust in his promise to save you, he considers that a full account of perfect, sinless righteousness—even though those are not terms you'd use to describe your life. It's not righteousness you *earned*, but righteousness Jesus earned and gifts to you.

The example Paul uses of *logizomai* in action is Abraham (Romans 4:3). Abraham was a hundred-year-old guy who God promised would have a child one day with his ninety-year-old wife. But he still had no baby in his arms. So God said, "Go outside and look at the stars. That's how many descendants you will have" (Genesis 22:17, paraphrased).

Abraham looked up, and in that moment he believed God would do what he'd promised. He believed God even though it was clearly an impossible promise. Because of his trust, the writer of Genesis says, God credited Abraham with a completely righteous life, even though he had lived nothing of the sort.

In the same way, when you believe that God sent Jesus to die for your sins and make you his forever child, he credits you with a completely righteous life even though you have lived nothing of the sort. It's a gift you can only receive. If you're trying to earn it, it's not a gift. This is where so many people get tripped up before even starting the Christian life. They still think it is something they can *do* that makes them a child of God. Not only is that wrong, but it is bewilderingly depressing. You would always feel overwhelmed, not sure if you've done enough. Being overwhelmed gives way to exhaustion, and exhaustion gives way to despair. Then despair replaces any desire you have to know God with a resentment of him. You don't want to be close to him; you want to avoid him. And eventually, resentment turns to hatred.

The good news is that being God's child is something God gives you. Our place with God is not a hard-wrought position we earn, but a gift of grace accepted.

This is what separates the Christian message from every other religion in the world. Every other religion spells acceptance with God as *D-O*. *Do* good works. *Do* go to church, or mosque, or synagogue. *Do* keep the commandments.

The Bible spells acceptance with God not *D-O*, but *D-O-N-E*. It's not what you do that makes you a Christian, but what he's done that you receive.

But How Good Is Good Enough?

Maybe you do what many people do to make themselves feel good about their Christianity. They make up their own standard of goodness and congratulate themselves on meeting that standard. I call it "the good enough standard." Also known as "the standard of better thans."

I pray enough. I share my faith enough. I love my wife enough. Or . . .

I'm definitely better than the guy who just flipped me off from his Camaro with the Jesus-fish on the back. Or . . .

I'm pretty sure I'm one of the better moms in our large circle of friends.

I used to be like that. I naturally compared myself to the bargain basement types and felt pretty good about where I was in my relationship with God. But then I noticed a few problems.

Problem 1

There were enough people out there to whom I didn't compare well, which always had me worried. Our church would have missions Sunday, and I'd hear from the couple living in a hut in the Amazon who prayed for three hours every morning. And then I'd think, "I'm toast." The question "How good is good enough?" will always end in despair.

Problem 2

Even when I defined my own standards, I wasn't very consistent in keeping them. I found myself telling others "you should" and "you ought to" all the time. But in my own life, I didn't follow through on all the good advice I was dishing out.

Problem 3 (The Biggie)

God doesn't hold me up to my standards. He holds me up to his. And his "standard of righteousness" is Jesus Christ.

Uh-oh . . . But that's precisely where the good news comes in: "To the one who does not work but believes in him who justifies the ungodly, his faith is counted as righteousness" (Romans 4:5).

Romans 4:5 establishes three characteristics of a recipient of this gift:

- Characteristic 1: You know you are "ungodly." There is an inherent admission in what Paul says here. You know God requires thoroughgoing goodness, but your current state is far from it.
- Characteristic 2: "Does not work" means you do not think you can do anything to change your status. You've given up trying to earn God's approval.
- Characteristic 3: You "believe in him" [God] who promised to justify the ungodly himself.

Let me put that another way as a sort of confession:

- *I'm a sinner.*
- *And there's nothing I can do.*
- *Except to trust you to take care of that, God, just like you said.*

Those three confessions are why the apostle Paul said Abraham's faith was "counted as righteousness." And this wasn't just an Abraham thing. Paul continued: "But the words 'it was counted to him' were not written for his sake alone, but for ours also. It will be counted to us who believe in him who raised from the dead Jesus our Lord, who was delivered up for our trespasses and raised for our justification" (Romans 4:23–25).

In other words, "getting right with God" has nothing to do with your church attendance, prayer time, Bible reading, puppy petting, old ladies you've helped cross the street, degrees attained, or money given.

It has everything to do with believing in God who raised his Son, who died in your place for your sins, from the dead.

When we trust Jesus for our salvation and acknowledge him as Lord of our lives, God counts our belief as righteousness. When we accept Christ as our Savior, God *gifts* us Christ's righteousness.

Christians Aren't Perfect, but They Also Aren't "Just Forgiven"

When God gifts us Christ's righteousness, we're not just forgiven for the wrongs we've done. We also get Christ's perfect record credited to our account.

You see, Jesus was not just a dying Savior; he was a *doing* Savior. He lived the life we were supposed to live. God looks at us as if we've lived that perfect life. It's hard to wrap your mind around the idea, but in God's eyes, you get credit for all the amazing things Jesus did.

When God looks at J. D. Greear, he doesn't see how many times I've prayed, how sincere I've been in my faith, how many books I've written, how nice I've been to my mother-in-law (that's easy). . . . He sees Jesus's record. When I came before God this morning, he saw me as if I were so full of tenderness that I forgave those who were crucifying me. As if I had so much faith I walked on water. As if I had so much self-control I resisted Satan to his face after fasting in the wilderness for forty days. God sees me that way because when he looks at me, he sees Jesus. So in his eyes, I've had a really good day.

Grace, Grace, and More Grace

When it comes to getting right with God, we are as good as dead. We can't do anything to please, woo, bargain, or negotiate with God. Like an infertile Abraham and Sarah, we cannot birth anything good no matter how hard we try . . . and yet we were gifted righteousness. God sees you in the exact way he sees his Son.

You have nothing to offer God. God owes you zilch. He's not in debt to you.

It's only through his mercy (not getting what you do deserve) and grace (getting what we don't deserve) that you can be counted right with God.

Why would he do that? Love.

"For God so loved the world, that he gave his only Son . . ." (John 3:16).

Not love in response to our loveliness. Let's be honest: You and I aren't lovely people. (Me more than you) We've all battled our demons and wrestled with emotions. If we all tore off our masks at the same time, we'd be pretty horrified at how unlovely we all are.

And yet . . . *God*, before whom all things are "naked and exposed" (Hebrews 4:13), loves us. His eyes see all the dark shadows and hidden closets of each soul, sometimes with hate directed right at him—yet he loves us.

I don't understand it. I don't feel worthy of it. But I must believe it because Jesus said it. And I do. And now I see that believing in his love has produced the most incredible change in me. I want to serve God. I want to be close to him. I want to bring him pleasure. The sixteenth-century German reformer Martin Luther was right after all: God's love is not a response to our loveliness; his love creates loveliness in us. Our loveliness is a response to his love, not vice versa.[3]

So what is a Christian, exactly?

Let's go back to heaven's front gate, where God is asking you: "Why should I let you into heaven?"

A true Christian would answer: "I am not good enough to enter, but you sent Jesus to die for my sins. He said he

---

3. Martin Luther, "Thesis 28," paraphrased, Heidelberg Disputation, 1518.

came to save me, and I believed him. I submitted to him. I'm trusting him as my sin-bearer and entry rite into heaven."

And the gates of paradise will open wide.

Is that it? Is that all you have to say?

In one sense, yes. But it's more than just words here. This is not a magic incantation. There's a posture involved behind the words. Which brings me right back to my beloved *chair*.

Saving Faith Is a Posture, Not a Prayer

If I walked up to my most highly revered, beloved Chair of chairs and said to everyone listening, "I believe in this chair. I trust that it will hold my weight. I have full faith that this chair is sturdy and strong," *but then never sat in it*, you would wonder if I truly "believed" in that chair. We don't demonstrate our trust in chairs to hold us up by *talking* about them. We *show* our trust by plopping our weight down on them. If I truly believed in that chair, I would surrender my entire weight into the chair. Then I would sigh, restfully confident that the chair held me securely.

The act of trust (that is, faith) proves that we believe— specifically, that we "trust" that Jesus is Lord and show it by submitting to him, and that Jesus has done everything necessary to save us. He is our sole hope for heaven.

Without that kind of trust, our words are empty.

Obedience Is Faith in Action

In the book of Hebrews, faith is always synonymous with obedient actions and, on the flip side, unbelief with disobedience: "To whom did he swear that they would not enter his rest, but to those who were disobedient? So we see that they were unable to enter because of unbelief" (Hebrews 3:18–19).

One's belief, or lack thereof, is shown by where and how someone rests, surrendering their entire life. If you flip over to Hebrews 11, you'll find a roll call of the great men and women of faith in the Bible. What do we see from this? They all believed, and then they all obediently responded.

- Abel *offered*.
- Noah *built*.
- Abraham *left*.
- Jacob *blessed*.

Interestingly, in the Hebrew language, there is no noun for *faith*. *Faith* is only a verb, meaning it is always an action. You can't separate action and faith.

Just as I don't have faith in that chair unless I transfer my weight onto it, you cannot have faith in God without some physical, practical action that shows you believe.

In other words, we're talking about a *posture* here more than a specific *prayer*. The posture I take toward the chair, by fully shifting my weight toward it, shows my faith in that chair. The posture I take toward God reveals if I have fully surrendered my life to him or if I am holding back from surrendering to him.

It's a posture you start in a moment and maintain for a lifetime. The proof that you have adopted the posture is not how eloquently you can recount your decision to sit down. The proof that you adopted the posture is that you are sitting in the chair now.

Hebrews 3:14 tells us: "For we have come to share in Christ, if indeed we hold our original confidence firm to the end."

The true test of saving faith will be proven by its endurance, all the way to the end.

Which brings us to the "once saved, always saved" question. (A phrase never found in the Bible, FWIW.) I was taught that salvation was like a contract you signed with God, who wrote the date in permanent marker in his Book of Life. Done. Signed, sealed, deliverance.

That's not how the writer of Hebrews talks about it. He says we'll be saved if we hold on confidently, "firm to the end" (3:14). In Acts, when Paul and Barnabas were giving final words to a new group of converts, they urged them to "continue in the faith" because only by perseverance "through many tribulations we must enter the kingdom of God" (Acts 14:22).

Hold on, now. Are you saying we can lose our salvation?

Dramatic pause . . . for effect . . . just to make you doubt for a second.

No. Too many places in the Bible make it clear that you can't lose your salvation. In John 10:28–30, Jesus says that once you belong to him, nobody can "snatch" you away, which sounds to me a lot like the phrase "once saved, always saved." (So the phrase isn't in the Bible, but the idea is.)

On the one hand, you have the Bible saying that once God saves you, you'll always be saved; on the other, it says you'll only be saved if you endure to the end. Isn't that a contradiction?

Instead of pitting them against each other, put them together, which yields this: *One of the essential marks of saving faith is that it endures to the end.* How do you know if you're saved? Your faith holds on to Jesus (better: he holds on to you) until the very end of your life.

In three Gospels we read about Jesus's parable of the sower. He tells of a farmer who sowed some seeds with four dramatically different outcomes: birds ate some, rocks and shallow soil killed others, weeds and roots choked some more, and a few of the seeds grew abundantly into huge, beautiful plants. The apostles were confused by Jesus's meaning, so they asked for clarification. Jesus explained his parable like this:

"Hear then the parable of the sower: When anyone hears the word of the kingdom and does not understand it, the evil one comes and snatches away what has been sown in his heart. This is what was sown along the path. As for what was sown on rocky ground, this is the one who hears the word and immediately receives it with joy, yet he has no root in himself, but endures for a while, and when tribulation or persecution arises on account of the word, immediately he falls away. As for what was sown among thorns, this is the one who hears the word, but the cares of the world and the deceitfulness of riches choke the word, and it proves unfruitful. As for what was sown on good soil, this is the one who hears the word and understands it. He indeed bears fruit and yields, in one case a hundredfold, in another sixty, and in another thirty" (Matthew 13:18–23).

Question: Do the seeds in the parable that spring up quickly and then fade away represent saved people or unsaved people?

Answer: They represent unsaved people who, for a while, *look like* saved people. But the proof that they lack salvation is that they did not endure the sun of persecution and the weeds of temptation.

I've seen those little seeds of God's words tossed out at student camps, and I've watched countless teenagers walking forward, crying, pledging not to date until they're thirty, never to cuss again, to listen only to worship music, to memorize the entire New Testament in Greek and become missionaries to Afghanistan. Sadly, quite often, their commitment doesn't last past the bus ride home.

The evidence of true saving faith is not the intensity of emotions at the beginning but belief's endurance over time. The seeds in Jesus's parable that represent saved people are the ones that persevere until the end.

It's true, yes, that once you're saved, you're always saved, but it's also true that once you're saved, you'll be forever following God.

Assurance Comes from Your Present Posture, Not a Past Memory

A lot of people I know look back on some time when they were "saved" and wonder, *Did I feel sorry enough for my sins? . . . Was I truly repentant? . . . Did I understand enough about basic Christian doctrines? . . . Was I doing it for the right reason? . . .*

How do you know that you prayed the prayer right?

Let's go back once again to our beloved chair. I'm assuming that you're sitting down now while reading this. But how do you *know* you're sitting? Because you distinctly remember the decision you made to sit down? (Probably not.) Even if you don't remember making the decision to trust that chair, you obviously did it subconsciously. How do I know you made that decision? You're sitting now. You are a faithful chair-sitter.

It's the same with Jesus. Your assurance in Jesus doesn't come from a past memory when you prayed a prayer, got baptized, walked the aisle, filled out a card, or raised your hand with every head bowed and every eye closed. You may have *all* of those memories. You may have *none* of them. Either way, the assurance of your faith is what you're doing right now—your present posture before God.

The way to know you've "sat down" in Jesus is to ask yourself: *Do I trust him as my salvation now?* You can only be in one of two positions with the chair: standing next to it by the strength of your own legs or seated in trust on the chair. In the same way, you can only be in one of two relationships with Jesus: "standing" as lord and savior of your own life or "seated" in submission and trust in him.

Seated—I trust God and surrender fully to him.

Standing—I'm not so sure I can trust God, so I'll declare several areas "off-limits" to him.

Seated—I recognize God as my authority.

Standing—I am my own boss.

Seated—He has done everything necessary to pay for my sin. I accept that!

Standing—I must work hard at being good so God will let me in. I hope he grades on a curve!

Many people doubt their salvation because they can't remember when they prayed the prayer. But that doesn't matter. The question is: Are you seated in repentance and faith in Jesus *right now*? The way you know you made the decision to sit down is by the posture you are in now.

On the other hand, you may remember your prayer—as well as all the emotions wrapped up with it—but you are not currently in a posture of submission and faith. It just might be that whatever decision you thought you were making, you were *not* actually making. Your present posture, not your past recollection, is the best evidence of what you decided.

Your conversion puts you into a posture that you remain in for your whole life. If you are in that posture currently, then you made that decision previously.

So is it possible to be saved and backslide? In other words, can a Christian stand up from the chair and walk away?

All Christians wander at some point and think there's a better chair out there for them. Some even backslide down a slippery slope and struggle to climb back up the muddy mountain. King David committed sexual assault and murder, then lied about it for a year. So, yes, sincere Christians can backslide.

But David repented. Sincerely. He even wrote a song about it—Psalm 51—which has provided the language of repentance for countless generations of believers. David's salvation was demonstrated not by never falling, but by how he returned after he fell.

The evidence of our salvation is found in our resolution to return to the posture of repentance and belief. The Bible tells the stories of all kinds of failures—many who believed, then doubted, then believed, then sinned. Then believed again. The common theme is that they fell, but soon enough, they got right back in the chair.

Our assurance is grounded in our returns, not our falls. Believers will fall, but they always reassume the position of repentance and faith.

Conversion is not sinless perfection. It is, however, a new direction—a direction you stay oriented toward for the rest of your life.

Be Assured That God Wants You to Be Assured

What if I went away on a trip and said to my kids, "Daddy will be back soon . . . or maybe he won't. Maybe I'm not really your daddy at all. Maybe my real family lives somewhere else. You'll just have to wait and see if I come back. I might return from this trip with a gift for you, or I might not ever return. Sit around and think about that while I'm gone, and let that compel you to become better children."

Bad would not begin to adequately describe that kind of parenting. And if it's bad parenting, why would we think that's God's nature? Coercing us into good behavior by holding back assurance does not communicate love; it cultivates fear. The only way real love grows is through security. I don't need to tell you that. You know that already. You completely trust those you truly love with everything.

The Bible makes God's intentions for you very clear:

- "I write these things to you who believe in the name of the Son of God, that you may know that you have eternal life" (1 John 5:13).
- "We love because he first loved us" (1 John 4:19).
- Jesus said: "I will not leave you as orphans; I will come to you" (John 14:18).

- He also said: "If I go and prepare a place for you, I will come again and will take you to myself, that where I am you may be also" (John 14:3).

I could go on, but do you get the point? He's saying, "I love you. I won't leave you. I'm coming back for you." Once we have assurance, we then have peace, not fear, for: "There is no fear in love, but perfect love casts out fear. For fear has to do with punishment, and whoever fears has not been perfected in love" (1 John 4:18).

Love produces a whole new kind and a whole new level of obedience.

A completely new creation has new appetites and desires. You begin to seek God because you love God; to do righteousness because you crave righteousness. God is not just after obedience; he's after a whole new kind of obedience. An obedience that grows from desire, not fear.

You can express repentance and faith in a prayer, but the prayer itself does not save you; your repentance and belief lead to salvation. It is possible to repent and believe without praying, just as it's also possible to pray without repenting and believing.

So, if you've never done it before, have a seat. Put your feet up. *Trust*. Rest in your recliner because Jesus sits on the throne of your life.

2

What Are the Most Important Practices in a Christian's Life?

Let me start by asking another question: What is a zombie? Some of you could easily identify a zombie as a creature with a serious skin condition and a blank look on its face, that walks slowly with a limp, grunting and gargling, and sinks its teeth into people like it's bobbing for apples. That's probably a stereotypical definition and one I hope doesn't get me in trouble with ZombiesArePeopleToo.com.

Interestingly, zombies are the hot horror genre these days. The idea of zombies has been around for a long time but has resurged in recent years—some say due to cultural shifts in our world. I feel like the plot of every zombie show basically goes like this: "Hey, we need something from . . . yeah, over there, on the other side of town . . . just past *where the zombies* are."

Our day-to-day lives are like that. We want to get through our to-do lists and reach our goals, but we encounter mindless attacks. Emails and advertisements consume our souls. Tweets growl and voice mails hum low in our ears. We attack each one ferociously, only to see sixty-eight more popping up on the horizon. There's no end! They keep coming! We might be more prepared for the zombie apocalypse than you think.

Zombies are basically moving bodies without souls. They look like they are alive, but they're not.

Which could also describe some Christians. They shuffle through life—going to church en masse, grunting out some songs, then sucking the church dry with their many needs and complaints.

In the previous chapter, we answered the question of what a Christian is. We looked at the internal acceptance of the gift of salvation through a truly repented heart that fully surrenders to God. But is that all Jesus wants from us—to understand and believe in salvation by faith in Christ?

There has to be more.

CEOs

I love Christmas and Easter for many reasons, from the songs to the decorations to the piles of cookies that land in our staff kitchen. But I also love Christmas and Easter because those Sundays bring out the CEOs—those we at church affectionately call the "Christmas and Easter Only" crowd. It's *tradition* for them to go to church. They put on their holiday clothes, comb their hair, then waltz through our doors with a smile. They lap it all up while keeping an eye on that clock. Then, when time's up, they parade out, smiling away, greeting other CEOs they saw a year ago.

Honestly, I don't mind the CEOs. I'm glad our church feels like a place to come home to for the holidays. What gets me is when they try to identify as members of the Summit Church, tell others they attend here, then proceed to chew up, rip off, and stomp on people the other 363 days of the year.

All the while, people are thinking, *Those people go to the Summit?* I want to parachute in, shouting, "Yeah, but only at Christmas and Easter! I am only responsible for two days out of 365 for their behavior!"

The biggest problem, of course, is not what their behavior makes people think about me. It's what their lives make people assume about Jesus.

Which brings up another question: What does it really mean to live as a Christian? What are the essentials? Is adopting the posture discussed in the previous chapter enough? Is it that plus regular church attendance? Plus tithing and saying grace at mealtimes?

Tomorrow Is Another Day

If you are new to Christianity, something you may have noticed pretty quickly about Christian subculture is that we love bumper stickers. If you see someone with the whole back of their car plastered with bumper stickers, you know they are either a tree hugger or a born-again type. Or both. (Those people are always super interesting, but I try to avoid them. The granola-plus-Bible thing really intimidates me.)

Here are some of the worst ones I've seen.

- "This Fish Won't Fry! Will You?" (Confrontational evangelical Christian)
- "Are you following JESUS this closely?" (Passive-aggressive Christian)
- "CH__ __ CH What is missing? U R!" (Cheesy Christian)
- "Tithe If You Love Jesus; Anyone Can Honk." (Pastor's favorite Christian)[4]

Here's another one that's pretty popular: "Christians aren't perfect, just forgiven." (From my experience, people with those stickers are usually the worst drivers because they're asking you to pre-forgive them before they cut you off.) Part of that bumper sticker is true. Christians aren't perfect, but they are not *just* forgiven. Forgiveness is only part of the definition. They are also changed. They are followers of Jesus.

So, hypothetically, if you were to die tonight, yes, you would experience the forgiveness, grace, and mercy of God and enter heaven. But if you *don't* die tonight—and I hope you don't—what will you do, as a Christian, when you get up tomorrow?

---

4. Chris Boeskool, "The Unforgiveable Sin Of Bumper Stickers," *The Boeskool* (blog), December 5, 2013, http://theboeskool.com/2013/12/05/the-unforgivable-sin-of-bumper-stickers.

The basic definition of a Christian is a follower of Christ. Not a bad start. But here's how Jesus defined a follower—you'd better hold on for this one: "Then Jesus told his disciples, 'If anyone would come after me, let him deny himself and take up his cross and follow me'" (Matthew 16:24).

What does it mean to "take up his cross?"

For many Christians today, the cross is a delicate piece of gold jewelry they hang around their neck, or maybe even something they got tattooed on their shoulder. It churns up sentimental feelings of identity, sacredness, and belonging. But those sentiments are not what Jesus's original audience would have felt when Jesus said, "take up his cross." The cross was an instrument of shame. Torture. Oppression. Total defeat. Following Jesus means dying to everything in opposition to his will, forsaking all that he has forbidden. That was Jesus's requirement for someone to become his disciple.

As a pastor, I'm not *that* worried that most of my congregation will suddenly become raging, godless atheists. I am very worried, however, that many will never become disciples, satisfied instead to remain cultural Christians. *Christian* is a label you can attach to yourself that means all kinds of things these days, from the Christmas-and-Easter-only types to the Jesus-is-my-president type. Clearly, we need a simpler definition.

The first Christians did not even call themselves Christians. *Christian* was a name attached to them later: "In Antioch the disciples were first called Christians" (Acts

11:26). *Christian*, in fact, was a derogatory name that meant "little Christs."

What did these believers call themselves? It's right there: disciples. Did you know that the word *Christian* is only used three times in the New Testament, but *disciple* is used 281 times?

Maybe you wonder why I'm belaboring this distinction. It's because a lot of people who call themselves Christians are not really disciples. Biblically, there's no such thing as a Christian who is not a fully devoted, dead-to-self, cross-carrying disciple.

Remember Matthew 7:22–23? Jesus talked about a large group of people who, on the last day (his final return), will say to him (and I'm paraphrasing): "Lord, Lord . . . didn't we do lots of stuff in church and serve in kids' ministry, memorizing lots of verses and dropping twenty dollars every time the plate was passed? You know us, right?"

And he'll say, "Depart from me. I never knew you. You knew who I was and hung out at my house on the weekends, but I never knew you."

I bet you just sucked in a little air thinking about that one. He's talking to "Christians" with bumper stickers on their cars and everything! Many Christians are kind of like a celebrity entourage. They don't do anything but hang out with the star "in his name."

Acceptance and obedience cannot be separated when defining a true Christian. We're not accepted because we obey, but when we're accepted, we'll want to obey.

In John 14:23–24, Jesus tells us: "If anyone loves me, he will keep my word, and my Father will love him, and we will come to him and make our home with him. Whoever does not love me does not keep my words. And the word that you hear is not mine but the Father's who sent me."

God does not love you because you're a doer. He loves you because he loves you, and you become a Christian by accepting what *he has done* to bring you back to himself forever. But after that, you'll spend the rest of your life seeking to do for him as a response to the incredible thing he did for you.

He did. It's done. You do.

The Cure for Zombieism

The most essential component of the Christian life is becoming a disciple—seeking to live like Jesus lived.

If you're not doing that, then you don't belong to Jesus. You are just a zombie mimicking those who are alive.

If you're not yet a disciple, the good news is that you can become one (*right now!*) through a simple act of surrender. It's an immediate cure for spiritual zombieism.

God wants to put into you a power that will transform you from within.

Many think becoming a Christian means merely getting a fresh start and turning over a new leaf. It is that, but it's so much more. It's not just a new leaf; it's the power of a new life! You don't just receive a "get-out-of-hell-free" card. You get an "access-to-heaven's-power-on-earth" packet.

Even better news: this power transformed some of the most unlikely people into Christianity's greatest leaders.

- Peter—a coward
- Paul—a bully
- John—arrogant and vengeful

And yet, they changed the world. These three people and countless others were made from the same flawed material as you and me. It's not what you are able to do *for* Christ. It's what he can do *through* you, a fully surrendered disciple.

I really love baptisms. They are beautiful times, and I love witnessing someone doing a double-gainer with a twist just to get into the water. Then they splash out of the water like Shamu, ready to get to work serving Jesus. Just the other day, I was standing behind the curtain getting ready to step into the baptistry with five people who were making professions of faith. One of them was a fourteen-year-old boy, and as a joke, I told him if he'd cannonball in, I'd pay him $5. Without even hesitating, he did it. It was so amazing I paid him $20.

Baptism features that first step of obedience and the public profession of faith. You are telling others that you follow Jesus and want to be his disciple, under his authority. Symbolically, you go in the water as an old dead person, and you come out as a new alive person.

You are alive now to serve Jesus.

That means you have the ability to become his disciple. But what exactly is a disciple? As we've seen, you start with taking up your cross. But what comes after that?

Dude, Get Dusty

The word *disciple* had a broad usage in first-century Israel. Jesus wasn't the only one with disciples. If a young Jew admired an older mentor (often called a "rabbi") and wanted to become like them, they would go sit at their feet and learn of their ways. They would follow them everywhere, day and night, imitating them in all they did. What they ate. How they talked. Where they went. How they responded to various situations.

Christian historian Ray Vander Laan says that a first-century disciple was not someone who merely wanted to know what his master knew, but who also did all that his master did. The greatest compliment you could give to a disciple was to say, "The dust of your rabbi is all over you." That didn't mean, "Hey dude, it's time for a shower!" It meant that you were following your rabbi so closely that whatever he stepped in splashed up on you.[5] Wherever he was, there you were following right behind him.

At Summit Church, we define *disciple* according to five core identities that encapsulate Jesus's life and priorities. As you grow in these areas, you are growing in Christlikeness. People in our church love this framework for its simplicity, so maybe you'll find it helpful too.

---

5. Ray Vander Laan, *In the Dust of the Rabbi Discovery Guide: Learning to Live as Jesus Lived*, That the World May Know Series, vol. 6, Harper Christian Resources, 2015, DVD.

- Worshipers: A worshiper joins us for worship and understands the glory God deserves. They show up and are present with other disciples who are all surrendering their lives to Christ. *Immediate action steps: 1. Attend weekly worship at your church. 2. Have a set time every day to spend time reading God's Word and praying. If you don't know where to start, check out the devotional tab on the Summit Church app or try Lectio 365.*

- Family members: A family member joins our church family and designates our church as their home. Believers should be belongers. Church is not an event you attend but a family you belong to. *Immediate action step: Join a small group, Bible study, Sunday school class, or ministry team at your church.*

- Servants: A servant joins a ministry team and sacrifices their time and talents for the mission of God. They discover how God designed them and use their gifts for others in every dimension of their lives; from their job, their marriage, their neighborhood, and their church, they ask the question: "How can I serve you?" *Immediate action step: Join a ministry team at your church.*

- Stewards: A steward asks for what purpose God gave time, treasures, and talents and how they might invest them in the kingdom of God. Stewards recognize that what they have is a trust from God, not something they own, so they are generous in stewarding these gifts toward God's mission on earth. *Immediate action step: Start tithing at your church.*

- Witnesses: A witness actively goes out and tries to make more people into disciples. Their faith is contagious, and they can't help telling others about Jesus. We often say: we seek not just to be disciples but "disciple-making disciples." *Immediate action steps: 1. Identify one person God has put in your life who is not a Christian that you can pray for, love, reach out to, and share the gospel with. 2. Sign up for a mission trip at your church. 3. Use the Joshua Project's Unreached of the Day app to pray for a different group of unreached people around the world every day.*

As a person grows in each of these areas, we see the lights coming on in their eyes. They start to get it. Their faith is more than words. They really come alive.

It's beautiful to watch not just what the change does for Jesus and his church, but what it does to the people as they begin to see that the more they surrender, the more alive their faith becomes. Slowly, these former zombies discover the joy of living.

From Start to Finish, It's All About Surrender

Jesus didn't ask you to take up his cross and hang it on the wall over your kitchen table. Or take up his cross and wear it around your neck. He said to take up his cross and follow him.

The cross isn't meant to be decorative or sentimental. It's a symbol of the "death to self" we embrace to follow Jesus. Death to anything about your desires, dreams, or decisions that contradicts his.

As the quote often attributed to the German pastor-prophet-spy-martyr Dietrich Bonhoeffer says: "When Jesus bids a man to follow him, he bids him come and die."

Or think of it this way: Salvation is free; it costs us nothing. But following Jesus will eventually cost you something.[6] Maybe everything. At some point, as a follower of Jesus Christ, you will want to go one way, but Jesus will tell you to go another. That's when you'll discover if you've really embraced the cross.

Obedience to God will sometimes take you 180 degrees from where you want to go. But you go because you'd leave anything behind to hold on to him.

While growing up, I heard it expressed like this: In every heart there is a throne and a cross. If you are on the throne, Jesus must be on the cross. If he is on the throne, you must be on the cross.

So . . . who is on the throne of your life? Who is on the cross?

One of you must be on each.

---

6. Andy Stanley, "Don't Settle for Christian," sermon delivered June 14, 2020, Andy Stanley. https://northpoint.org/messages/don-t-settle-for-christian.

It's Scary but Worth It

Deciding to fully follow Jesus is a little bit like giving someone a signed blank check. (For those of you under thirty-five who don't know what a check is, it's a piece of paper authorized by the bank to transfer money from one person's account to another.) Giving someone a *blank* check means they have the ability to fill in whatever amount they want. The check giver has said yes to whatever amount they ask for before they even ask for it.

Following Jesus means you hand your life to Jesus as a blank check, saying, "All I am . . . all I have . . . all I ever hope to be . . . I surrender all. It's yours. You fill in the blanks whenever and however you want."

And then, with him as your rabbi, you seek to live like he lived, care about what he cared about, prioritize what he prioritized, and pursue what he pursued. You're going to get divinely dusty.

Jesus saved you, you see, so you could be like him. He wants not only to take you to heaven but also to put heaven into you. He wants to use you as his representative on earth in each of the five areas listed above.

I love the way my friend David Platt once said at a conference: "Jesus didn't save you to disinfect you and put you on the shelf; he saved you to put you into service."

The defining characteristic of the Christian life is the decision to fully follow Jesus, whenever and wherever, living by faith in his finished work at the cross and in the resurrection, seeking to continue the work of redemption and restoration that he started on earth.

That commitment will express itself in you becoming a worshiper, family member, servant, steward, and witness, just as he taught and modeled for us.

No zombies allowed.

3

How Can I Discover My Purpose on Earth?

I love the *Lord of the Rings* movie trilogy that came out between 2001 and 2003. (I also love the books, but this isn't the place for the book-versus-movie debate. They're both awesome.) Just about everyone is familiar with LOTR, but it takes a special kind of fan to watch the extended cuts of all three movies. I know a few people who have done this *in succession*. We're talking eleven hours and twenty-six minutes.[7]

There are so many great character dynamics in J. R. R. Tolkien's classic, but the relationship that stands out is between the two main hobbits, Frodo Baggins and Samwise Gamgee. (Um, need I say, "spoiler alert"? I mean, honestly, the books have been out since 1954 and the movies since the early 2000s, so if you haven't read or watched them yet, I don't see how that's on me.) Frodo has a dangerous ring that

---

7. I have to imagine that by the time those people reach the credits—after listening to the music and absorbing the strange ways New Zealanders spell their names—they may be wondering if these actors really are from Middle-earth.

everyone wants, and his mission is to throw it back into the huge volcano (Mount Doom) from whence it came. Sam's job is to help his friend accomplish his mission.

Toward the end of the second movie, *The Two Towers*, Samwise makes an iconic speech at a low point in their adventure.

> It's like in the great stories, Mr. Frodo. The ones that really mattered. Full of darkness and danger they were, and sometimes you didn't want to know the end. Because how could the end be happy? How could the world go back to the way it was when so much bad had happened? But in the end, it's only a passing thing, this shadow. Even darkness must pass. A new day will come. And when the sun shines, it will shine out the clearer. Those were the stories that stayed with you. That meant something, even if you were too small to understand why. But I think, Mr. Frodo, I do understand. I know now. Folk in those stories had lots of chances of turning back, only they didn't. They kept going. Because they were holding on to something."[8]

Samwise recognizes that life is a story that will one day be told—it will mean something—as long as people don't give up and keep going forward. Hardship, disaster, and toil

---

8. *The Lord of the Rings: The Two Towers*, directed by Peter Jackson, 2002 (Montréal: New Line Home Entertainment, 2011), DVD.

end some stories too soon, before their purpose has been clearly fulfilled. But hardship, disaster, and toil make other stories more engaging, meaningful, and purposeful as the main characters conquer and achieve their mission.

So many factors in the past few years have impaled people's desire to discover their purpose. Suicides have increased dramatically over the past two decades, with "purposelessness" leading the list of causes. Quite shocking to me was the fact that suicides have also increased among our military, police, and first responders. If any lives are characterized by purpose, they would be those of these men and women.[9] And yet they, like many of us, struggle to find purpose.

Samwise gave this speech over halfway through the trilogy, at a point when they had already been through some harrowing life-or-death moments. Had they given up then, claiming their task was too tough to continue, the story would've been over. Roll credits. You'd have been sitting in your theater seat, shrugging, and mumbling, "That's it?"

The events of life can make you doubt if there's meaning and purpose in your story, but they don't have to if you're looking for the bigger picture. Amid the turmoil, Samwise saw the bigger picture.

---

9. Sally C. Curtin, Matthew F. Garnett, and Farida B. Ahmad, "Provisional Numbers and Rates of Suicide by Month and Demographic Characteristics: United States, 2021," U.S. Department of Health and Human Services, National Vital Statistics System, September 2022, https://www.cdc.gov/nchs/data/vsrr/vsrr024.pdf.

Isolation and fractured relationships cause people to wonder if they matter. We can blame COVID-19, political division, social media, or cultural trends for their impact. Through it all, we need a friend like Samwise to encourage us to move on—to remind us that we matter and that our lives have meaning.

God sees the bigger picture. Your story is longer than eleven hours and twenty-six minutes. You could be fifteen years old, sixty-seven years old, eighty-nine, whatever the director determines.

He wants you to know you have a purpose and your story matters. Like Samwise said, you can find something to hold on to.

You Were Created for a Purpose

If you're in your teens or twenties, you're probably making plans for your future and asking this question: "What is my purpose?" Like many, you probably equate "your purpose" with "your job."

At this point, I'm supposed to say something like, "No, your job is only what you do to pay the bills. It's not your purpose! Your purpose is to go to church and sing worship songs."

But believe it or not, your job can be a big part of your personal purpose. Part of being made in God's image, in fact, is being created for work.

When God created the first humans, Adam and Eve, he made them stewards of his creation. You see, God made the earth incomplete; the book of Genesis says God looked over what he had made and said it was "good" (Genesis 1:31). Good is good, but good is not perfect. *Perfect* means something cannot be improved upon; *good* means the raw materials are all solid, but there's potential for more work to be done.

For example, if you met my wife out in public, you'd think she was perfect in every way—her hair, makeup, clothing—with everything in its place; she's a perfect ten in every category. When I wake up next to her every morning, she's . . . well, good.

God put Adam and Eve into a world with gardens that needed cultivating, buildings that needed building, and supply chains that needed organizing. He made us his regents—or you could say cocreators—in helping shape a planet beautiful in form and useful for humans.

That means the work that we do—whether paid or unpaid, glamorous or mundane—glorifies him. Have you ever considered what it means for your work to please God?

I think of a story from 2004 involving an American Airlines pilot who, in his preflight announcements, asked all the Christians on board the plane to raise their hands. He then suggested that during the flight the other passengers talk to those people about their faith. He also told passengers he'd be happy to talk to anyone who had questions. Understandably, it freaked out a lot of people: the pilot of your airplane talking to you about whether or not you're ready to meet Jesus?[10] Like many Christians, he thought that serving God at his job meant using his job to evangelize. I'm all for more evangelism, but flying passengers safely from point A to point B also pleases and glorifies God. To work is to partner with him in his stewardship on earth.

God created you with special gifts, talents, interests, and passions that guide you to his specific purpose for you.

When God placed Adam in the garden of Eden, he didn't just tell him to keep away from certain bad apples. God placed Adam in the garden "to work it and keep it" (Genesis 2:15). Remember that God said this *before* the curse of work, indicating that work wasn't a punishment inflicted on Adam for his sin. It was a part of God's original design. The first purpose God had in mind for Adam wasn't to read a Bible or pray, but to be a good gardener.

The Hebrew word translated as *work* shows what God means. The word is *abad*, and it connotes preparing and developing, as in creating. Adam was placed in the garden to develop its raw materials, to cultivate a garden. Christians can fulfill their created purpose in the same way, by taking the raw materials of the world and developing them.

Architects take sand and cement and use them to create buildings. Artists take colors or musical notes and arrange

---

10. Tracy Sabo, "Pilot's proselytizing scares passengers," *CNN.com*, February 9, 2004, https://www.cnn.com/2004/TRAVEL/02/09/airline.christianity/.

them into art. Lawyers take principles of justice and codify them into laws that benefit society. It's satisfying as well as meaningful to create just like God creates.

Work is our first commission by which we serve God. The Bible declares that even the most menial jobs have an essential role in the mission of God (Colossians 3:23).

I had a great model of this growing up. My dad and mom were the strongest Christians I knew. My dad was not a pastor but a businessman, managing a Sara Lee plant in Winston-Salem. (Oh, the desserts he brought home!) My mom taught biology at a local college. My first awareness of Christianity was from people who applied their faith to their jobs in the so-called "secular" sector. They worshiped God by doing their work excellently, with integrity, and as an act of service to others.

In fact, it is surely not coincidental that most of the parables Jesus told had a workplace context, and of the forty miracles recorded in the book of Acts, thirty-nine occurred *outside* a church setting. I tell the people at Summit Church that for someone like me working in the church, that means I only have access to one-fortieth of the power of God. Most people think of the power of God as something experienced in church. I hope you experience it there, but the *primary* place we see it displayed in Scripture is through God's people in the surrounding community.

Throughout Acts, it's much easier to find the apostles out in the workplace than to find them in a church. The workplace is where God wants to display his power. The

God of the Bible seems as concerned with displaying his power outside the walls of the church as within it.

A lot of people think making a business "Christian" means attaching some cheesy Christian name to it. For example:

- Leaven and Earth Bakery
- A Cut Above Hair Salon
- Garden of Eat'n Restaurant
- Holy Grounds (or He-Brews) Coffee Shop
- Cane and Able Mobility Healthcare Clinic

Glorifying God in your work is more than just hanging a sign on a business. A Christian's job is to bring God's presence to the world. God is active through a person's work to ensure that families are fed, homes are built, and justice is carried out. Too many Christians begrudge their work when they ought to revel in the fact that God is using them, in whatever small part, to fulfill a greater purpose.

This also applies to those who work in the home. The home is God's incubator of love and encouragement. At home, moms, dads, and kids all discover something about themselves they may not have known previously. Families shape us and develop us, while we shape and develop each other. Through every crisis and victory, you discover your God-given purpose together.

My wife and I have always loved the story Tony Campolo used to tell about what his wife, Peggy, who stayed home with their four children, would say when someone asked her what she "did." She would say, "I am socializing two Homo sapiens into the dominant values of the Judeo-Christian tradition in order that they might be instruments for the transformation of the social order into the kind of eschatological utopia that God willed from the beginning of creation."[11] Then Peggy would ask the other person, "And what do you do?"

For many of us, our job becomes our platform from which we can share the gospel. Maybe not so much like that American Airlines pilot did, but in and through the relationships our jobs enable. This, ultimately, was how Paul worked. Was Paul a tentmaker (secular) or a church planter (spiritual)? Yes and yes. Paul pushed the gospel farther out into the world than anyone else of his time, yet he worked a "secular" job to support himself as he traveled and proselytized.

Another great example comes from the Academy Award–winning movie *Chariots of Fire*. The biographical movie follows the Christian track athlete Eric Liddell during his preparation for the 1924 Olympics. At one point in the film, Liddell is confronted with an objection to his career, since there are more pressing matters in life for a Christian than merely running. Liddell responds, "I believe God made me for a purpose, but he also made me fast. And when I run, I feel his pleasure."[12] At some point or another, while you

---

11. David Baggett, "Reflections on *Why I Left, Why I Stayed*, by Tony and Bart Campolo, Part 2," Moral Apologetics, October 6, 2021, https://www.moralapologetics.com/wordpress/whyileft2.

12. *Chariots of Fire*, directed by Hugh Hudson, written by Colin Welland, 1981 (Burbank, CA: Warner Bros., 2010), DVD.

worked at something you love or are good at, you may have had a similar feeling—*This is what I was made for.*

Ephesians 2:10 tells us, "For we are his workmanship, created in Christ Jesus for good works, which God prepared beforehand, that we should walk in them." Yes, you were created to work, but Paul also sees that "work" as "good works." You can do good works at work or at home, school, or church. You can fulfill your work by doing whatever God created you to do for his glory and as a testimony to him.

Let's unpack a little bit more what that means.

You Were Created to Be Excellent

Bill and Ted were not the first to say, "Be excellent to each other." (If you were born after 1990, I know you have no idea what I'm talking about. YouTube it.)

People in my generation thought Bill and Ted made up that line, but God said it through Paul in the book of Colossians.

If our work is done for God, then it should be done according to the highest standards of excellence. Paul says, "Whatever you do, in word or deed, do everything in the name of the Lord Jesus, giving thanks to God the Father through him" (Colossians 3:17). That should be true whether or not we receive any reward for our work, and whether or not anyone even notices our efforts.

Let's be honest—it is demoralizing to work for someone who doesn't give us credit for what we've done, or worse, only ever responds by offering critical feedback. A bad boss can make otherwise satisfying work an absolute terror. In a situation like that, most people lose the motivation to work with excellence. They may think, *What is the point of working hard? No one will notice either way, and even if they do, I certainly won't get the credit for it.* It's understandable why someone would think that, but a Christian knows better.

Christians ought to pursue excellence in their work—not because they want to impress their boss or because working hard leads to better pay, but because they work first for Christ. I've always attributed this thought to C. S. Lewis, who noted how valleys undiscovered by human eyes are still filled with beautiful flowers. For whom did God create that beauty if no human eyes would ever see it? Lewis's answer was that God does some things for his own pleasure. He sees excellence even when no one else does.

This perspective adds new significance to *every* task a believer performs, even if the believer knows they will never be recognized. They no longer require the approval of others in their work because they no longer work primarily for others. They work first for Christ, and he deserves their best.

Remember when God worked at creation? Everything he did was called "good." He does good work. I wonder if Jesus's carpentry skills were appreciated when he worked on earth. There's no way he produced shoddy stuff. He definitely would have received five stars on Angie's List.

A Christian with a poor work ethic or sloppy academic performance gives the world a terrible testimony of Christ. That person may say with their mouth that "Jesus is Lord," but when they don't care to turn in assignments on time or respect the boss, they are saying even louder, "I myself am lord." When working with excellence, Christians not only serve God but also display an attitude of service to the world.

Martin Luther said: "When we pray the Lord's Prayer, we ask God to give us this day our daily bread. And he does give us our daily bread. He does it by means of the farmer who planted and harvested the grain, the baker who made the flour into bread, the person who prepared our meal."[13]

Gene Edward Veith adds to Luther's premise in a great little book called *God at Work*:

> We might today add the truck drivers who hauled the produce, the factory workers in the food processing plant, the warehouse men, the wholesale distributors, the stock boys, and the lady at the checkout counter. Also playing their part are the bankers, futures investors, advertisers, lawyers, agricultural scientists, mechanical engineers, and every other player in the nation's economic system. All of these were instrumental in enabling you to eat your morning bagel. . . . Though [God] could

---

13. Martin Luther, Luther on Vocation; as paraphrased in Gene Edward Veith, *God at Work: Your Christian Vocation in All of Life* (Wheaton, IL: Crossway, 2002), 13.

give it to us directly, by a miraculous provision, as He once did for the children of Israel when He fed them daily with manna, God has chosen to work through human beings, who, in their different capacities and according to their different talents, serve each other.[14]

That truck driver stuck in traffic may not see his purpose, just the traffic. The warehouse workers may just see stacks of boxes after a long day, not the purpose. What *is* their purpose? To feed the world! That means God is present in the world through secular vocations—both for believers and nonbelievers alike—providentially caring for humanity.

Rethink your job, career goals, talents, and passions. See them as gifts to create life and health for others and glory to God in the process. If work for you is just about making money, you'll fail to see the excellence.

So go find a job that you love to do, that you can do excellently, where you feel God's pleasure and benefit others.

That's step one in finding your purpose.

But there's a second step too.

You Were Created with a Mission

The start of every *Mission: Impossible* movie finds Ethan Hunt (played by Tom Cruise) opening a package with instructions inside about his mission. He learns the who, what, where,

---

14. Gene Edward Veith, *God at Work*, 13–14.

when, and why. It will be a tough mission (one might even say *impossible*), not for the faint of heart, and only Ethan and his team can get it done—by driving a hundred miles per hour through crowded streets while exchanging coolheaded, witty banter with the good-looking, perfectly manicured people riding along with them. You know, relatable stuff.

We have a mission, too, spoken by Jesus himself and delivered to us through Matthew: "All authority in heaven and on earth has been given to me. Go therefore and make disciples of all nations, baptizing them in the name of the Father and of the Son and of the Holy Spirit, teaching them to observe all that I have commanded you" (Matthew 28:18–20).

This assignment, the Great Commission, is given to every Christian, and it centers on one thing: making disciples. For every single Christian everywhere, these words are at the heart of who they are and what they do.

How do you make disciples? You need to "go." Well, technically, you already *are* going. The verb in the Greek literally means "as you are going." It assumes you're headed somewhere already. *As you go* through life. *As you go* to work. *As you go* to school. *As you go* to the coffee shop. Everywhere you go, there are people who need Jesus.

Your work is a mission field, providing access to so many people around the world. You don't have to hop on a plane to Zambia, because Zambia may show up at your Starbucks. England may appear on your Zoom call, or Brazil on WhatsApp. Christians today are able to gain more admittance than ever to strategic, even unreached places. Globalization, revolutions in technology, and urbanization have given the business community nearly universal access. Before he died, Billy Graham said the next Great Awakening in America would likely happen in the workplace.[15] That's where some of you head every morning at eight o'clock.

What if you saw that God had shaped you intentionally, giving you gifts, talents, and experiences that would put you in certain places where you could share the gospel with those who would otherwise not hear it? The apostle Paul told the Athenians in Acts 17:26 that God determines the borders of various peoples so that people groups everywhere could learn to seek God. What God does with nations, he does with individuals as well. Your personal borders have been determined so that somebody, somewhere, could learn to seek God.

For many of you, your skill in something will be what gains an audience for the gospel. Proverbs 22:29 says, "Do you see a man skillful in his work? He will stand before kings." Let your skill and excellence in your work take you before the kings of the earth, and when you get there, tell those kings about Jesus.

My friend Mike is a world-renowned brain surgeon at one of the country's leading university hospitals, which happens to be right here in North Carolina. Every year a

15. https://www.globaladvance.org/stories/awakening-the-sleeping -giant

group of doctors from all over Asia comes together to hear him lecture on the latest developments in the field. He starts each set of seminars with his testimony of how he came to Christ and an explanation of how the gospel shapes his view of medicine.

I once asked him, "But doesn't your very secular university object to that? And what about the Buddhist and Muslim doctors? Don't they object?" Mike smiled and said, with a twinkle in his eyes, "They never really say anything. I mean, what can they say? I'm the best in the field right now, and they respect what I do." You may not be a brain surgeon, but like Mike, you can do your work with such skill and excellence that it gains a ready hearing for the Savior for whose glory you do it.

Let me hasten to add here: Like Mike, some of you have secular skills that can give Christians access to countries that would otherwise swiftly reject their presence. I realize I'm talking to a small subset of people, but it's an important subset.

The countries most in need of a gospel presence are those in the so-called "10/40 window," which refers to the area of the globe between ten degrees south and forty degrees north of the equator. These regions are home to nearly four billion people, almost half of whom may have never heard a word of the gospel. Spanning sixty-nine countries, the 10/40 window is home to millions of the world's impoverished people, as well as many of the world's adherents to non-Christian religions (such as Islam, Hinduism, Buddhism, and Atheism).[16]

Years ago I read that if you were to add up all the Christian missionaries from every denomination in the 10/40 window, that number would come to forty thousand. That's a lot! And praise God—we need four times that many. But do you know that the number of Americans working in (so-called) secular jobs inside the 10/40 window right now? Two million. Around 35 percent of those working in such jobs call themselves "born-again Christians." If even a third of those Christians were serious enough about their faith to see their primary calling in life as "disciple-making disciples," that would mean an extra two hundred thousand missionaries. Can you imagine increasing the mission force in the 10/40 window more than *fivefold* without costing the church a dime?

These wonderful but spiritually lost places in the world need both the words of the gospel and the tangible reflection of God's love that some businesses can provide. Millions in this region are without work and without the knowledge of Christ. For some of you, or for one of your children, maybe that's your purpose.

One example, though dozens could be provided, is the nation of Iran. As a country, Iran is an unreached area

---

16. "The 10/40 Window," Window International Network, accessed June 22, 2023, https://www.win1040.org/about-the-1040-window.

in desperate need of the gospel. As of May 2021, out of
84 million people, only 13.4 million Iranians hold full-
time jobs.[17] How are places like this to be reached? Iran
can be reached through the efforts of average Christian
businesspeople taking their skills and expertise overseas.
This may not be the path for every Christian, but perhaps
God is challenging you to consider leveraging your work for
his mission-advancing purposes.

Not every Christian, of course, will be led to perform
work in an unreached region. That's a unique opportunity
for some. But disciples of Jesus should always do their work
with a view toward the Great Commission. A "missional
vision" for Christian work is to do it well, and to do it, if at
all possible, somewhere strategic.

Again: "Do you see a man skillful in his work? He
will stand before kings; he will not stand before obscure
men" (Proverbs 22:29). Believers who do their work well
can be greatly used in the work of the Great Commission.
Their excellence in business can give them audiences with
the "kings" and influencers among the most unreached
peoples in the world. Your (so-called) secular skill might be
the key that opens up some nation or people group to the
gospel. Missionaries talk about the 10/40 window, but for
businesspeople, that window is a door. So, do your work,
but don't forget the mission.

---

17. Bahram Khodabandeh, "Number Crunching: The Truth Behind
Iran's 'Single-Digit' Unemployment Rate," IranWire, May 14, 2021,
https://iranwire.com/en/features/69545/.

The mission is more important than everything.

It's like my dad always told me: "Son, only two things in life last forever—the Word of God and the souls of people. Make sure you build your life around both."

I gave an example once during a sermon, calling five people onstage and assigning each a different role on a make-believe fire truck.[18] One was the driver, another the supervisor, and the others operated the hose, assisted with the hose, and drove the back of the truck (the tiller). When I asked each of them what their primary responsibility was, each person clearly knew their role but forgot their mission:

To put out fires.

We focus on our specific role but forget the overall mission all the time—to make disciples of all nations.

God is interested in how Christians do their work, and he wants to be involved in it. Your work can make an eternal difference in the lives of those you work with, those you work for, and those you serve through your job. Allow the gospel to transform the way you look at and do your work. You were redeemed by grace—now live out that grace in the context of your job. You may never look at work the same way again.

In addition to going, *teaching* is an essential part of the Great Commission. Most teaching happens not in classrooms but as you walk through life with someone

18. I got the idea from David Platt, who did a similar demonstration during one of his sermons.

and show them how to serve God and apply his truth to relationships, disappointments, joys, losses, failures, and victories. Wes Smith, the college pastor at our church who is also one of the best disciple makers I know, says, "Eighty percent of discipleship is informal. It's spending time with people. Discipleship is living ordinary life with gospel intentionality."

What Is Your Purpose, Really?

God has a very personal purpose for you. It starts by realizing he's given you a particular stewardship over part of his creation.

God's purpose for you is about serving others, making disciples of them, and sharing the story of Jesus with them.

He wants to be glorified through you. That's why everything you do must be done with excellence. The ultimate center of all that happens on earth is to give glory to God.

His purpose is for you to surrender your dreams, job, talents, and gifts to him to fulfill that purpose.

That's what he has called you to do.

How do you find your personal purpose in life? You start by finding work you love, then use it as a platform to reach others for Christ and do it with excellence.

It will not be easy. Every mission field has dangers and setbacks. (Paul can confirm that.) But what a story your life will tell!

If you do these things, then as the last chapter of your story is written, you'll look back and see that your life had meaning and purpose.

I love the scene in C. S. Lewis's *The Lion, the Witch and the Wardrobe* in which "Father Christmas" gives each of the four displaced children a mysterious gift. Though they don't know it at the time, these gifts will prove essential in the coming battle with the White Witch and her minions. For example, in the heat of battle, Lucy realizes that her gift, a healing ointment, must have been given to her to bind up the wounded because she sees the need all around her. Peter realizes his sword is meant to lead an assault on the White Witch. In that moment, they perceive what Aslan—the lion representing Jesus—wants from them.

In the same way, we come to know more about what God wants from us by reflecting on the gifts he has given to us—whether they be spiritual gifts or natural gifts.

Finding your purpose begins with God's Word—discovering what he is doing on earth, the chief of which is giving every person a chance to hear the gospel. It continues by looking within yourself at the specific gifts he has given you, communing with him in prayer to discern his will for your life, and plugging in to the body of Christ so other saints can give you wise counsel.

He's got a specific purpose for you, and you'll never feel fully alive until you find it.

4

If God Is Really in Control, Why Is There So Much Evil and Suffering?

A devastating earthquake hit Turkey and Syria in February 2023, resulting in the deaths of more than 56,000 people, damaging or destroying at least 230,000 buildings.[19] Rescuers reported that the stench of death filled the air for weeks after the incident.

On April 20, 1999, two shooters entered Columbine High School in Colorado and killed thirteen innocent people and injured twenty-four more. Then they turned the guns on themselves. That event touched off a string of shootings for decades in malls, stores, places of worship, and even in elementary schools, such as Sandy Hook, where twenty-six people died, including twenty children between the ages of six and seven years old.

---

19. "2023 Turkey-Syria Earthquake," Center for Disaster Philanthropy, updated August 23, 2023, https://disasterphilanthropy.org/disasters /2023-turkey-syria-earthquake/.

Jeffrey Dahmer killed seventeen men and boys between 1978 and 1991, dismembering them and *eating* them. John Wayne Gacy killed thirty-three young men and boys, then buried them in his basement. He loved to entertain children as Pogo the Clown.

The 9/11 attacks on the United States in 2001 left 2,996 people dead. Lives were shattered and buildings destroyed, triggering a series of repercussions whose effects are still felt today.

The world leader with the most deaths credited to his name is Mao Tse-tung, who was responsible for the deaths of around forty-five million of his own people between 1958 and 1962. That exceeds the total number of deaths caused by Hitler and Stalin combined.

How is it possible that God is in control?

Is God not powerful enough to stop violence, or does he just not care?

Some, trying to maintain belief in a good God amid such terrible things, posit that God is just as bewildered as we are but can't do anything because he's given us free will and is bound to honor his decision. That's the theme of movies like *Bruce Almighty*. "You can't mess with free will," an exasperated Morgan-Freeman-looking-God tells Jim Carrey as they discuss the state of the world.

Believe it or not, the only way to find peace in this question is not to conceive of a God who is less in control of human events, but more.

We Like a Small God

Philosophers call the problem of seemingly unjust suffering in the world "the problem of evil." The challenge was often attributed to the Greek philosopher Epicurus in the fourth century BC, and for twenty-five hundred years now it has been expressed like this: If God is all-loving and all-powerful, why do terrible things happen? If God were all-loving, he would want to stop terrible things. If he were all-powerful, he *could* stop terrible things. Thus, the fact that terrible things are still happening means that God is either not all-powerful or not all-loving. Or, more likely, that God does not exist.

Admittedly, it's a pretty tough argument to respond to, but its layers are missing a crucial premise: If God is infinite in love and power, would it not also follow that he is infinite in wisdom? And if his wisdom is as high above ours as his power is above ours, should we expect to be able to understand his ways?

Think with me for a minute: How much power would it have taken to bring this universe into existence?

Astronomers estimate there to be two hundred billion trillion stars. That numeral looks like this: 200,000,000,000, 000,000,000,000. With *twenty-three* zeros.

Now, if you're like me, numbers in the millions, billions, trillions, or septillions tend to sound all the same after a while, so let me show you this trick to help you remember the difference between million, billion, and trillion.

One million seconds ago. Do you know what you were doing a million seconds ago? That's about eleven days ago. I was watching my son's tennis match. The opposing kid's parent and I were the only ones watching, and we were trying to cheer for each of our kids without being obnoxious. I felt really awkward when my son won in a tiebreaker and couldn't even make eye contact with the other parent.

What about a billion seconds ago? Do you remember what you were doing then? That would be thirty-one years and eight months ago. Some of you can't remember what you were doing a billion seconds ago because there was no "you" to speak of. A billion seconds ago was sometime in the early 1990s. Bill Clinton had just been elected president. The first website was created. *Forest Gump* was eating chocolates on a park bench.

How about a trillion seconds ago? How long ago do you think that would be? A couple centuries back? Nope, keep going. A trillion seconds ago would be 31,709.8 years. (*Rocky 1* had just been released.)

Now think about the fact that there are at least two hundred billion trillion stars, each one putting out roughly the same amount of energy as a trillion atom bombs every second. Some are so big they defy description—like Eta Carinae, a stellar system within our own Milky Way that is five million times brighter than our sun.

Stars exist in an expanse we simply cannot comprehend. The Hubble Telescope is now sending back faint infrared images of galaxies we didn't even know about, estimated to be twelve billion light-years away—meaning that if you hopped in a spaceship traveling 186,282.2 miles *per second* (the speed of light), it would only take you twelve billion years to get to them. (Unless you have a layover in Atlanta, which almost always doubles your travel time.)

Astronomers speculate that once you got to those galaxies, you'd likely see a few billion more light-years' worth of stars ahead of you from there.

All of this was created by God simply saying, "Let there be light."

Now, let's compare that to *our* power: I can't lift my mattress over my head. (Almost didn't make it because I tried.) I have a rowing machine at my house that measures how many "watts" I am generating. When I'm at my max, killing it at a pace I can sustain for about thirty seconds, I generate about 350 watts—enough to power a small dorm room refrigerator for about two minutes. That's the highest output of my power. Maybe you're in better shape than I am, but I bet you can't put out a great deal more than that.

So here's the question: If God's wisdom is as high above mine as his power is above mine, how can I not conclude that some things are beyond my ability to understand? This conclusion means it is entirely possible that God is working out beautiful purposes we just can't see yet.

A famous skeptic named Bart Ehrman teaches at UNC-Chapel Hill and lives not far from me. Dr. Ehrman was preparing for ministry but then lost his faith because of the presence of what he calls "purposeless evil," but there is a huge assumption behind his words.[20] It's this: If there *is* a purpose, *he'd* be wise enough to detect it. But isn't it rather arrogant to assume that, despite our limited knowledge, we would be able to perceive every purpose of an infinitely wise God?

You see, as I said above, our core problem is that we don't think of God as that much bigger than us; we only think of him as a slightly bigger, slightly smarter version of us.

But does that make any sense when we think about how big God would have to be to pull off creation?

God is not just big; he's beyond all of our categories for big. He's so big we cannot exaggerate him.

The God of the Bible is the opposite of small and manageable. British philosopher Evelyn Underhill is credited with saying that a god small enough to be understood will never be big enough to be worshiped.

Here's the irony: We want a small God capable of sustaining our faith, encompassing the mysteries of our existence, and igniting our passion. But only a *huge* God can do all those things. The problem is that a huge God scares us. (Good! He should.) We can't control or manipulate him (and we shouldn't). He doesn't serve us; we serve him—the only appropriate way to relate to a God of this size. That's why the writer of Proverbs 1 says: "The fear of the LORD

---

20. Bart Ehrman, *God's Problem: How the Bible Fails to Answer Our Most Important Question - Why We Suffer* (San Francisco: HarperOne, Revised, 2009).

is the beginning of knowledge; fools despise wisdom and instruction" (1:7).

Without a trembling awe before the majesty of God, we will never really know him. If we don't know him, then we doubt him because we've shrunk him down to our size.

Without a trembling awe before the majesty of God, we can't help but doubt him. If we fear God, then we know exactly who God is.

Which is exactly what happened to Job.

Job: The Poster Child of Evil and Suffering

We don't know a lot about Job. We don't know when he lived. The book doesn't say. We don't really know *where* he lived. The book says Uz, but scholars don't have much more of a lead on where that is than you or I do. Do you follow a yellow-brick road to get to the land of Uz?

What we do know about Job is that he was "blameless and upright" (Job 1:1). There aren't many people, even in the Bible, described like that. Job was a good dude. He loved his mother, ate his vegetables, and turned in his library books on time. He read every word of the "terms and conditions" on his new iPhone updates before accepting them. All in all, a really stellar fella.

After we meet him, the scene cuts to heaven where God is having a staff meeting. Yes, heaven has meetings. And one of God's "staff" has crashed the party—a feisty one named Satan, which in Hebrew means "the accuser" or "prosecutor."

He says, "You know, God, the only reason people serve you is because it's in their own self-interest. They serve you because you give them stuff. Let them suffer when their stuff is taken away and they'll give you up." (I'm paraphrasing here.)

God smiles. "Okay, let's use Job as a test case. Take away everything in his life that he loves, and you'll see that he values me for me."

Satan squeals, "Oh goody," then proceeds to do just that. He takes everything from Job that matters to him—his business, his home, his kids, his health . . . but not his wife. (Honestly, I'm not sure what that means. She does turn out to be a bit cranky, so maybe that explains it.)

So at this point, you're supposed to jump out of your seat and cry, "Wait, what? Why in the world did God allow pain and suffering to happen to such a decent guy?" We read the rest of the book to find the answer to this question. But that's not what happens.

Job's friends show up. They sit with Job for days, mourning with him in silence like good friends would do, before things go off the rails. They try to find answers to Job's suffering by making him feel even more miserable in his misery.

"Look, we know God is just," the friends say. "And we know everything happens for a reason. So the fact that you just lost everything means you did something wrong. What was it? You can tell us."

Job pushes back. "No. I mean, I'm not perfect, but I'm innocent of anything that would warrant this."

"C'mon, Job. You've lost everything. There has to be something. Think hard. We'll wait."

"I'm telling you. I'm a pretty good guy."

"You're not thinking hard enough, Job. What did you do yesterday?"

This goes on for thirty-seven chapters. Job maintains his innocence while his friends assume his guilt.

Then God shows up . . . to give answers to the issue of evil and suffering? No. He offers more questions—sixty-four of them, to be exact. Things like:

- "Job, what did you think about the laws of physics I created to undergird the universe? Do you even know what they are?"
- "What were you doing when I put the constellations together?"
- "While we're at it, where do storms come from, and can you predict when they are coming?"
- "Job, how much do you know about the reproduction habits of goats?"
- "Why are ostriches so darn weird?" (Not kidding: Job 39:13—paraphrased, of course.)

Why does everything suddenly shift to a press conference with Job on the stage and God rapid-firing impossible questions? God's supposed to be on the hot seat, not Job.

God shifts the conversation to show Job that he's not approaching this conversation from the right perspective. God is saying, "Dude, if you can't fathom all the mysteries behind these natural things, are you really in a place to understand the reasons behind pain and suffering?"

Job's friends have puny assumptions about Job's situation. To say, "Job, you are bad and God is mad," is simpleminded of them. God's ways and our ways are not the same. His ways are bigger. Bigger than big. Septillion big. He's saying, "If you don't understand constellation placement, goat reproduction, and ostrich weirdness, then you don't have any right to hold court with me."

Then by chapter 40, God's like, "Do you really think you can run this world for a day?" Think about it—God engineers the lives of eight billion people at the same time, which is like playing eight billion games of chess, moving and countering their free wills to create infinite possibilities that impact each other's games. And every game ends as God allows it to end.

Finally, as the story concludes, God drops the mic and Job drops to his knees. God supernaturally spanks Job's friends and gives Job back everything he lost, seven times as much.

If you've read the book of Job, then you've probably held the Bible in your hand and thought, *What just happened?*

I believe the book of Job makes five crucial points about the size of God to help us understand who is really in control. Spoiler: It's not Satan, evil, or suffering.

1. God's Power Is Sovereign[21]

Many scholars would agree that Genghis Khan was the most powerful king of all time. He was born in AD 1162, unified Mongolia, and pushed his empire east across Asia to the Pacific, then west to the Adriatic Sea into the area of Italy and Greece, and finally north into Russia. Through his genius and discipline, he turned a tiny nomadic tribe into a terrifying war machine.

There's just one problem: Genghis died in 1227. While his sons carried on the Mongolian empire for over one hundred years, it fizzled in 1368.

God rules over every nation, kingdom, empire—the entire universe, the seen and unseen, the earth, and all the planets. He rules over his army of angels, and he rules over his enemies, the demons, and even Satan. In fact, Satan has to ask God for permission at a meeting to do anything, even if it's only to make one guy's life miserable.

God does stuff all over the world—in the sea and above the mountains, in places we don't even know exist,

---

21. David Platt, "Our Suffering and God's Sovereignty: The Life of Job," *Radical* (podcast), February 11, 2019, https://radical.net/ podcasts/radical-podcast/our-suffering-and-gods-sovereignty/. Some of my points here are indebted to an excellent sermon on this passage by David Platt. These are the four points he made:

    1. God's sovereignty means God is great in power.

    2. God's sovereignty means God's purpose is guaranteed.

    3. God's sovereignty means that his knowledge is perfect.

    4. God's sovereignty means his mercy is personal.

in places that seemingly have no impact on you and me. Job 38:26 says God turns on the sprinklers to water a land nobody lives on. I forget to water my own yard, and I see it every day.

2. God's Perspective Is Infinite

In the 1939 film *The Wizard of Oz* (note: not the Wizard of Uz, who was Job's uncredited magician friend), Dorothy and her friends enter the throne room of the Wizard, whose voice booms out as they approach:

> Oz: "I am Oz, the Great and Powerful! Who are you? Who are you?"
>
> Dorothy: "If you please, I—I am Dorothy, the small and meek. We've come to ask you—"
>
> Oz: "Silence! The Great and Powerful Oz knows why you have come."[22]

The Wiz then chastises them for bothering him and questioning him. Finally, he agrees to their demands for a brain, heart, and courage but says they must prove themselves worthy by accepting a challenge—bring him the broom of the Wicked Witch, which obviously he can't do himself.

---

22. *The Wizard of Oz*, directed by Victor Fleming, 1939 (Burbank, CA: Warner Home Video, 1999), DVD.

Dorothy and Toto tremble at his voice, and that scene gave me, as a kid, the smallest taste of what it may be like to stand before an infinite, all-wise, and all-powerful God. Of course, unlike with Dorothy, this voice does not come from a small man hiding behind a curtain. This voice belongs to a God who is bigger than his voice—and his voice is the power that brought all of creation into existence out of nothing. This is a God who is before all things, understands everything, and knows the end from the beginning.

The word we use to describe this characteristic of God is *omniscient*, meaning all-knowing and all-seeing, from every possible perspective.

> For my thoughts are not your thoughts,
>> neither are your ways my ways, declares
>> the Lord.
> For as the heavens are higher than the earth,
>> so are my ways higher than your ways
>> and my thoughts than your thoughts.
> (Isaiah 55:8–9)

I do a really good job seeing things from my perspective. I'm not as good at seeing things from my wife's perspective. Even less so at seeing things from God's. God sees everything, all the time (past, present, future), from the most mundane (goat birth) to the most important (death). That also includes the day you rammed your toe into the leg of the coffee table. Best believe he heard the word that came out of your mouth.

God didn't create all this world, check off his God-Do list, wipe his hands, and move on. No, he watches everything, down to the most minute details nobody else cares about or even knows about. God remembers what happened during each and every trillionth second that has passed on this earth and beyond. I'm stumped over what I had for breakfast this morning. God knows what I had and what eight billion other people had for breakfast. The second that just passed while you read that sentence? God knew what eight billion people were doing, and he'll never forget it.

Job realizes God's perspective and immediately apologizes: "Therefore I have uttered what I did not understand, things too wonderful for me, which I did not know" (Job 42:3).

The smartest thing Job does is admit how limited his knowledge is.

3. God's Purposes Are Guaranteed

Satan woke up one morning (yeah, I know, go with me on this one) and said to himself, "I think I'm going to take God down." So he showed up at God's ten o'clock Angelic Roundtable Meeting and decided to challenge God right in front of Gabriel, Michael, and all the archangels.

Maybe there was a stunned gasp, then everyone held their breaths. "Did he just challenge God?" they asked each other. God, unwavering, accepted the challenge, then through the entire book of Job proved Satan wrong. Not only did God prove him wrong, he used Satan's whole scheme to advance his own purposes. Satan's attacks yielded a book that has provided encouragement to countless believers through the centuries, including you and me today.

Obviously that's not what Satan planned. But it's what God planned.

This happens all the time in Scripture. God uses evil, tragedy, and setbacks to advance his purposes.

- "Oh no, the Egyptian army is chasing us, and we're stuck between them and this uncrossable Red Sea!"
- "Good gracious, this giant Goliath is unstoppable!"
- "We're doomed! Our friend Jesus is dead, and they sealed him up in a tomb!"

Throughout the Bible, God repeatedly takes the worst days and uses them for the best purposes. He still does. Don't you have a story in your own life that shows God working in mysterious, behind-the-scenes ways? (A breakup set you up for a healthier relationship; the cancer made you appreciate what really matters in life; the season of infertility made you more understanding as a friend, etc.) If you and I, given our limited perspectives, can already see some of God's hand in difficult seasons in our lives, how much more would we see if we understood what he sees?

British journalist Malcolm Muggeridge put it well:

Contrary to what might be expected, I look back now on experiences that at the time seemed especially devastating and painful, with particular satisfaction.

Indeed, I can say with complete truthfulness that everything I have learned in my seventy-five years in this world, everything that has truly enhanced and enlightened my existence, has been through affliction and not through happiness.[23]

Affliction is God's opportunity to reveal himself. As Romans 8:28 tells us, "We know that for those who love God all things work together for good, for those who are called according to his purpose."

Make sure to note what that verse *doesn't* say. It doesn't say suffering is enjoyable. If someone sees suffering as pleasurable, they should probably schedule an appointment with a therapist. But—and Job realized this—even the bad things will *work together* for good with God at the helm. We may not see all the ways that is happening now, but I bet you can already look back on *some* of the painful moments of your life and see how they yielded something good. If, with just a little bit of time and perspective, you can *already* see a purpose for some of the pain, don't you think, given infinite time and God's perspective, you'll one day see God's good purpose in all of it? I love how John Piper says it: "God is always doing 10,000 things in your life, and you may be aware of three of them."[24]

---

23. Malcolm Muggeridge, as quoted in John Piper, *Desiring God* (Colorado Springs: Multnomah, 2011), 265–66.

24. John Piper, "God Is Always Doing 10,000 Things in Your Life," *Desiring God* (blog), January 1, 2013, https://www.desiringgod.org /articles/god-is-always-doing-10000-things-in-your-life.

Let me offer some good purposes that may apply to your suffering. (Not all of these will apply in each situation, and there are others not in this list.)

1. Your suffering caused you to open your ears to the voice of God.
2. Your suffering brought others into a deeper relationship with God.
3. Your suffering brought you closer to your family, your spouse, or others.
4. Your suffering caused you to get involved, start a ministry, or help others.
5. Your suffering gave you a testimony to help others going through something similar.
6. Your suffering shaped you to be more like Jesus.
7. Your suffering made you love Jesus more.

There's an old mansion not far from where I live called the Biltmore House. Adorning the walls are these massive, breathtaking tapestries. Tens of thousands of intricately woven individual strands, coming together to form a perfect picture in which not one strand is out of place. But if you flip the tapestry over and look on the backside, you might see a jumbled mess. Seemingly random threads going every direction. Chaos. Right now, our lives feel like we're on the jumbled mess side. But one day God will flip over the tapestry of history, and we'll see that not one thread was out of place. God was weaving together every event in our lives into a beautiful picture of Jesus—both in us and in the world.

I always tell our church they can understand three of God's biggest purposes in our suffering by looking at the three Old Testament "Joes":

- Job (JOE-b): Suffering helps us understand and love God more.
- Joseph (JOE-seph): Suffering helps us save others.
- Jonah (JOE-nah): Suffering chastises us and puts us on the right path.

Joseph, the son of Jacob, was elevated to Pharaoh's right-hand man. After guiding the nation through a seven-year famine, he understood why his brothers threw him into a pit and sold him as a slave, which turned into years in a prison until God promoted him from prisoner to vice president overnight. He said to his brothers: "As for you, you meant evil against me, but God meant it for good, to bring it about that many people should be kept alive, as they are today" (Genesis 50:20).

It took some time for Joseph to understand that what Satan intends for harm, God intends for good. But eventually he did. If you are a believer and currently suffering, God has a good purpose for you. If you love him, trust him, and listen to him, one day you will understand.

4. God's Promises Are Everlasting

My favorite verse in Job, hands down, is Job 19:25: "For I know that my Redeemer lives, and at the last he will stand upon the earth."

Here's why I love that verse. Let's break it down piece by piece.

- "I know": I love Job's assurance.
- "My Redeemer": the one who takes garbage and turns it into gold.
- "Lives": God is alive and paying attention.
- "At the last": the final chapter, when everything is said and done.
- "Will stand upon the earth": God will win victoriously.

Job lives that truth in chapter 42. He gets everything he lost back in the end.

Will you get everything back you lost in the end? Heaven is that place. Samwise in Tolkien's *The Return of the King* famously referred to a place where everything sad will come untrue.[25] Not only will all we lost be restored to us, but we'll also see that God was working through our temporary loss for our greater good. I also know that those who love and trust the Lord will enter eternity and receive perfect joy—in the end.

> You make known to me the path of life;
> > in your presence there is fullness of joy;
> > at your right hand are pleasures forevermore.
> > (Psalm 16:11)

---

25. J. R. R. Tolkien, *The Return of the King* (New York: William Morrow, 1994), 951.

In the resurrection, death is swallowed up in victory, and we experience the fullness of joy. "Fullness of joy" means joy that could not get any stronger; "pleasures forevermore" means joy that could not last any longer.

That promise gives you the ability to enter that joy now. Your eternity has already begun. Your life on earth is a brief ellipsis (. . .) compared to the expanse of heaven.

C. S. Lewis, a man familiar with pain, said, "If you think of this world as a place intended simply for our happiness, you find it quite intolerable: think of it as a place of training and correction and it's not so bad."[26]

Despite how your life's current headlines may read, it won't be this way all the time. Remind yourself of the everlasting promises of God.

5. God's Presence Is Pledged

Moses spoke the following words to the people of Israel as they prepared to face their enemies and take over the land of promise: "Be strong and courageous. Do not fear or be in dread of them, for it is the LORD your God who goes with you. He will not leave you or forsake you" (Deuteronomy 31:6).

And Jesus spoke the followings words to his disciples as they prepared to face opposition and spread the gospel:

---

26. C. S. Lewis, "Answers to Questions on Christianity," Question 5, *God in the Dock: Essays on Theology and Ethics*, ed. Walter Hooper, 1970.

"Behold, I am with you always, to the end of the age" (Matthew 28:20).

In both instances, the followers faced adversity, failed, rose to victory, lost, and gained ground—and God was with them every step of the way.

God's presence doesn't promise painless results, at least in the short run. It certainly doesn't promise a path of ease. But it transforms our experience of pain. His presence promises that he will be with us until the end. I'm not sure about you, but when I've suffered, what torments me most aren't the unresolved questions but the feelings of loneliness. It's not just, "I'm in pain," but, "I'm in pain and no one gets it; no one cares."

God's presence speaks to that fear. At times life may hurt badly and everything may feel out of control, but God is with you and working. He's not limited by time or threatened by Satan's attacks. He created the universe, and he sees you in it. Not only is he watching, but he relates.

You may feel pain. So did Jesus.

You may feel alone. So did Jesus.

You may feel betrayed. So did Jesus.

There is a lot about suffering I don't understand. But the cross shows me one thing my suffering *can't* mean: it can't mean God has forsaken me, forgotten me, or failed me. No matter how dark your days, the empty tomb shines light into your life. In your pain, you have his presence.

Corrie ten Boom and her sister Betsie suffered horribly in a Nazi prison camp. Corrie remembers her sister saying,

"We must tell them that there is no pit so deep that He is not deeper still."[27]

Steve Saint, whose father was murdered on the beaches of Ecuador by a hostile tribe, returned to the tribe, made friends with his father's murderer, and led him to Christ. He said: "Why is it that we want every chapter to be good when God promises only that in the last chapter he will make all the other chapters make sense?"[28]

Through Job's story, God shows us this: His *power* is sovereign; his *perspective* is infinite; his *purpose* is guaranteed; his *promise* is everlasting; and his *presence* is pledged. (Sorry, I'm a Southern Baptist preacher. I love alliteration.)

The story of Job is not an answer to the question of why so much evil and suffering exists. It's a revelation of who God is, which we need when we face evil and suffering.

Job's sufferings are actually quite mysterious, and even God's purposes are hidden from him, his friends, and the book's readers. And yet out of Job's agony and suffering comes one of the most profound revelations of God's nature in the Bible and indeed in all of literature.

You don't need an explanation of God's ways; you need a *revelation of who God is*. You don't need answers as much

27. Boom, Corrie, John Sherrill, and Elizabeth Sherrill. 1920. *The Hiding Place*. New York, NY: Bantam.

28. Steve Saint, "Sovereignty, Suffering, and the Work of Missions," *Desiring God*, Desiring God (blog), October 8, 2005, https://www. desiringgod.org/messages/sovereignty-suffering-and-the-work -of-missions.

as you need his presence. You need a God who is so big that you can rest in him.

That's why Jesus came—so you could know the intimate presence of that God, his friendship, and his rest for your soul.

Is God in control? Yes. Is there evil and suffering in the world? Yes.

Just because evil and suffering exist doesn't mean God has lost control. The cross and resurrection assure you of that. He's working it all for good, so that for those of us in him, all our crosses end in resurrection just like Jesus's did.

Allow evil and suffering to reveal just how awesome God is, and let them drive you closer to him. And never forget: He is right there with you. You aren't alone.

It may not feel like it right now, but God is up to something good in your life. That's what the cross and resurrection assure you of. And your God is big enough that when it's all said and done and you get to see it from his perspective, you'll understand how it was all working infallibly for his glory and your good. Each strand of your life has been woven together into cords of perfect love.

God is big enough to pull that off, and that's why he alone is big enough to be worshiped.

5

Isn't the Bible's Morality Outdated?

Ah, the eighties.

We used to talk on a phone nailed to the kitchen wall with a fifty-foot-long curly cord that doubled as a jump rope. We had to memorize phone numbers. (I still remember the number of my home that I grew up in, but I'm not sure I could accurately give you the number of my best friend's current cell.)

People dropped by unannounced. When you heard an unexpected knock on the door, you didn't call 911 while loading shells into your shotgun. We would talk to whoever randomly stopped by, even solicitors who wanted to sell us a vacuum. They might want an iced tea.

Malls were amazing. The social and cultural apex of every happening city. Malls were what you did on Friday night.

Going into malls now feels spooky. Scattered individuals and teams of elderly speed-walkers. Gigantic parking lots now filled with Amazon delivery vans.

Back then, dogs were not allowed in restaurants. Smoking was, but there was a section for smokers, and you had the choice to sit in it. Secondhand smoke was not a thing. If you wanted to listen to music, you carried a radio the size of a large suitcase down the street, usually on your shoulder.

Music, of course, was at its zenith. Rock bands would slash through their guitar solos and light their drum sets on fire. If the music was really good, somebody would smash a three-thousand-dollar guitar onstage to make the point.

UNC men's basketball won the NCAA championship in 1982 because of the steady hand of a rising star named Michael Jordan. Rocky Balboa proved to everyone that you could take innumerable blows to the head and still emerge victorious. Indiana Jones discovered treasure all over the world, Ralph Macchio put bullies in their place, and Tom Cruise protected us from Russian aggression high above an unnamed sea. (Come to think of it, some of these things have never left us.)

Whenever I'm especially hopped up on a heavy dose of nostalgia, I have one conclusion: the eighties were good.

But were things *actually* better back then? Many people felt no shame saying they disagreed with mixed-race marriages, and several states felt free to fly the rebel flag above their capitol buildings. When something called AIDS wreaked havoc on America, many labeled it God's judgment on the homosexual community so we ought not seek a cure. Sexual abuse victims were roundly ignored, even villainized.

CNN and MTV pioneered twenty-four-hour, constant-contact, media-intake overload.

People permed their hair. **Shudder.**

All of this was merely *forty years ago*. No wonder the Bible, written thousands of years ago, is accused of being outdated. Our views on morality change by the year. Why in the world would moral views from millennia past matter to *us*?

Last Decade Is Ancient History

I get this question about the Bible a lot, especially on college campuses and especially when it comes to questions of sexuality. Our society has been in a sexual revolution since the 1960s, where yesterday's taboos have become today's pride. What was considered normative in the 1980s would today be considered narrow-minded and bigoted, and I imagine what is normative today will seem out-of-date in just another decade.

I try to explain to these students that just because the Bible offends them today doesn't mean it's wrong. Many things that offended our ancestors we now appreciate.

For instance, the Bible's insistence on the equality of the races offended American slave owners in the 1700s, which is why "slave Bibles" routinely omitted the book of Exodus and large sections of the New Testament. Don't want those slaves getting any ideas about equality. Elizabeth Cady Stanton offended a generation and spawned a revolution by publishing a book-by-book analysis of the entire Bible showing that the whole thing pointed toward women's rights and equal suffrage. Offensive in one generation; enlightened in another.

I served for a period in a Muslim country. When I talked to my friends there about sexual ethics—that marriage was intended to be one man and one woman for life, etc.— they would nod their heads in agreement. Then I would say that God wants us to forgive those who have sinned sexually, and they would start shaking their heads. "No, no, no, that's not possible," they would say. "If forgiveness is given to the adulteress or the homosexual, then society itself will unravel."

The Bible offends *every* culture, just in different ways. It is, as the late Tim Keller often put it, an "equal-opportunity offender."

Culture changes fast—faster now than in the past— and it still seems to be accelerating. Those celebrated on social media yesterday are canceled today. And here I am, in the midst of that rapidly changing culture, saying that an ancient book offers the definitive view on modern life. Why would I say that?

First, a little humility is in order. If we look back at some of the things our grandparents believed, we might shake our heads and say, "I can't believe educated people could have believed that." But remember, they felt the same way about *their* grandparents. Do we really think it likely that our great grandkids will look back at us today and think, *Wow! Now, they really had it all together. So wise. So advanced.*

No. They will undoubtedly think, *Man, how in the world did they think what they did? What kind of monsters were they?* Some of what they'll critique I can already imagine: our propensity to look inside ourselves for guidance, our gender-bending surgeries, our gruesome removal procedures of babies from the womb, our relentless pursuit of luxury when some people were still living without clean water. Likely there will be another dozen things we consider normal now that they will consider barbaric and backward—just as we look back at the practice of American slavery and find it indefensible. It's scary to think about how harshly future generations will judge us.

As our culture changes by the minute, the Bible sits there stubbornly, unchangingly, unflinchingly claiming to be God's standard of right and wrong for all time. Why take its claims seriously?

Ultimately, of course, I take it seriously because it is God's Word, and God has the moral authority to declare right and wrong. Multiple things attest to the Bible's divine origin— fulfilled prophecy, the resurrection of Jesus, the beauty and uniqueness of the person of Jesus, among others. This is not the place to press deeply into all the reasons you should trust the Bible—simply to say that the *most fundamental* reason we trust the Bible is because we believe it was authored by God.[29]

---

29. For further reading on this topic, check out N. T. Wright's *The Resurrection of the Son of God*, Neil Shenvi's *Why Believe*, Richard Bauckham's *Jesus and the Eyewitnesses*, or Tim Keller's *Reason for God*. Also, Josh and Sean McDowell have some great YouTube videos summarizing the evidence.

We don't have to stop there though. Throughout my decades as a pastor, I've found several other truths that have helped me see the Bible as the most revolutionary, progressive-in-a-good-way, conservative-in-a-good-way, and enlightened source on morality known to humanity.

You Say You Want a Revolution?

The Bible has been behind the greatest moral revolutions in history. Let's take one example—slavery. Many rightly ask how Christians could have participated in, and even promoted, slavery. Good question.

The sad reality is that almost every major culture in the world practiced slavery. Sociologist Thomas Sowell points out that the European slave trade trafficked eleven million Africans between the 15th and 19th centuries. Yet twice that many were bought and sold on the Arabian Peninsula during the same time period, and every slave sold into the European slave trade was captured and sold by other Africans, who profited off their own people.[30]

The point in bringing this up is not to lessen the wickedness of the European slave trade, but to show that slavery has been endemic to almost every major human civilization in history. Sinful humans leverage their power

---

30. For more about this, check out Thomas Sowell's three-volume Culture series: *Race and Culture: A World View, Migrations and Cultures: A World View, Conquests and Cultures: An International History.*

to manipulate and exploit others, and slavery is one of the many manifestations of that.

Sowell also points out that while most civilizations practiced slavery, the only ones to push for abolition were Christianized nations. Those who called most vocally for abolition in the United States were Christian preachers and teachers. Christian society produced reformers like William Wilberforce, John Wesley, and Frederick Douglass. These abolitionists and many others pointed to Christian teaching as the basis for their calls for reform.

And just consider: the transatlantic slave trade was abolished *against* the objections of African and Arab countries. Slavery wasn't fully and legally abolished in every African country until 1981.[31]

Jump ahead a bit: what about the revolution of civil rights for Black men and women? It is no accident that Martin Luther King Jr., *a Baptist preacher*, called for the end of segregation in the US. Or that apartheid ended in South Africa thanks to Archbishop Desmond Tutu, *an outspoken Christian*. All of these leaders spoke from a worldview shaped by biblical convictions.

The women's suffrage movement in America, too, was entirely grounded in the biblical idea that men and women are created equal. We tend to take that for granted now. A hundred years ago, people didn't. But the *biblical* ideal

---

31. John D. Sutter, "Slavery's Last Stronghold," *CNN.com*, accessed May 31, 2023, https://www.cnn.com/interactive/2012/03/world/mauritania.slaverys.last.stronghold/index.html.

was clear: women are made in God's image, worthy of the same respect and dignity as men. Still today, women are not seen as equal to their male counterparts in many countries, except Christian ones. As noted above, the document that women's suffrage leaders used to propose the idea of male and female equality was . . . wait for it . . . *the Bible*.

Science and technology have done many wonderful things for our society, but science and technology have not spawned our most important moral revolutions. Quite often, they've been behind our worst atrocities.

Nine out of Ten Atheists Agree

I once listened to a lecture by Dr. Charles Mathewes at the University of Virginia, and he said that most atheists today who have moral objections to Christianity don't realize they are "Christian atheists," which means that the basis for their objections usually comes from teachings that have been shaped by a Christian worldview.

Friedrich Nietzsche, my favorite atheist, also acknowledged this. He said his moral objections to Christianity ultimately came from the principles he learned from Christianity. One historian notes: "Atheists today aren't like they were 1,000 years ago. They are Christian atheists."[32]

Many atheists are confounded by the fact that if you go anywhere in the world where the need is greatest, you're

---

32. Jeremiah Johnston, *Unimaginable* (Bloomington, MN: Bethany House, 2017), 17.

likely to run into Christians. There's definitely something about the Christian faith that compels believers to get involved in the worst situations on the planet.

Why would people work in horrible conditions to help those most marginalized, forgotten, and helpless? The Bible. People read the moral imperatives found in those pages, discover God's love for the world, and go out to do something to change and save lives.

Consider this: up until a few years ago, every single hospital established in Sub-Saharan Africa was built by Christian missionaries.[33]

Or take the issue of sex trafficking. Turning little children into sex slaves is morally repulsive, but it's still a common practice. Today, many of those on the front lines or in the trenches to fight sex trafficking say they do so because of what they read in the Bible.

Christians are working around the world, almost always without fanfare, to eradicate poverty, to promote equity among men and women, to build infrastructure, to heal the sick, and to offer dignity to marginalized people, such as those living in leper colonies. I could go on and on and on. The point here isn't to say that Christians are inherently good people. Nope. We're messed up. But the *book* we've got has a way with

---

33. David Toole, "The Role of Mission Hospitals in African Health Systems: Case Studies from the Nile River." Duke Global Health Institute, https://globalhealth.duke.edu/projects/role-mission-hospitals -african-health-systems-case-studies-nile-river-basin.

us. It pushes us outside our comfort zones, leading us toward beautifully radical displays of compassion and sacrifice.

A lot of the trouble we have with the morality of the Bible comes from reading it too sloppily. We see a rule here or there that doesn't sit well with us, so we toss out the whole thing.

But we need to remember that the Bible is primarily a *story*—a story that takes place in the mess of human history—and that God's revelation didn't happen all in one big moment. The theological term for this is "progressive revelation." It means that for some things, the further along in the story we go, the more clarity we gain on the morality God intends.

God initially legislated his nation Israel with rules on the outside pushing in (the Old Testament pattern). Then Jesus showed up and did not advocate a new nation based on God, but rather a new way to affect nations from the inside—by planting seeds in the hearts of people that eventually grow to undo injustice and promote equality.

Take, for example, the issue of polygamy. Many critics point out great Bible "heroes" like Abraham, Isaac, Jacob, and David who practiced polygamy, while the Bible never condemns them for it. But read those passages more closely. When the Bible talks about polygamy, it always ends badly. Then Paul, in the New Testament, points out that the reason polygamy is a bad idea is because God's original design for marriage was one man and one woman bound for life, as demonstrated in the first book God ever authored—Genesis.

Here's another example: Abraham, Isaac, and Jacob routinely practiced the cultural tradition of prioritizing the firstborn son. It was an unfair and unjust system, leaving the family fortune to one child at the expense of others. Where is the Bible's condemnation of that? You won't find a direct condemnation, per se, but you will see that God consistently chose the younger son, or the weaker one, for blessing. Jacob, not Esau. Joseph, not Reuben. David, the youngest of Jesse's sons, not Eliab, the tallest and strongest. God undermined the system of the rights of the firstborn son by instituting a gospel that favored the overlooked and protected the vulnerable.

Why not make the condemnation more immediate and direct, you ask. I've heard many say they wish Paul and the apostles had been clearer in their calls for societal reforms, of which the Roman world needed many—things like the importance of accountable government, the abolition of slavery, the principles of just war, and equitable systems of punishment. It's true, Jesus and the apostles didn't *lead* with those reforms, even though they taught the principles that would one day lead to them.

Here's why: if the apostles had made those reforms the focal point of their message, hearers might have latched on to those things at the expense of the very gospel that made such reforms possible. God changes societies like he changes individuals—from the inside out, by changing values and worldview assumptions.

God called his church to preach the gospel. But (and this is a big but) in that gospel were the seeds for every great and noble reform our society needed to experience.

It's All There in the Gospel

The gospel is the greatest equalizing force in the world. Christ teaches that in him there's neither Jew nor Greek, neither slave nor free, neither man nor woman, and neither young nor old, but that we're all one in Jesus (Galatians 3:28). The gospel is still miles ahead of our most progressive thinkers.

That doesn't mean we should accept every new trend that calls itself progressive as from God. It's really easy for our thinking to go wrong. We must tether our values to the commands found in the Bible. Forget about being on the right side of history; make sure you're on the right side of God's Word.

Society submits timely mores to timeless truths. What we thought was bodacious and tubular in the eighties got overrun by what was jiggy and buggin' in the nineties. Now, if I'm hearing the kids right, we want things that slap and slay.

It doesn't much matter what our society is saying right now—about sexuality, about the nature of freedom, or what it means to be true to ourselves. God isn't fazed. He has seen enough history to know where we're actually headed. And as the one who *made* each one of us, he knows how we work best. He gets right and wrong because he is, in his essence, the standard of righteousness. He invites us to share his perspective on what is good and bad because he is, in his essence, a good, good Father.

So when the next trend washes through our culture, don't have a cow, man. Be chill and go to the Bible for some totally gnarly guidance. (Right? People still say those phrases, don't they?)

6

Why Isn't God
Answering My Prayers?

There's a new form of rejection in our electronic age.
You know. It's probably happened to you.

You sent a text, and you got left on "read."

As in, they read your text and didn't reply.

You went out on a limb, shared an interesting obser-
vation or a link to a funny blooper video, and days later,
no reply.

You got ghosted.

It's even worse when you share something funny or
meaningful on a thread with twenty people and *no one*
replies. It's the digital equivalent of saying something at
a dinner party and everyone stopping and staring at you.
Total cyber silence. Not even the crickets are cricking.

A simple "Liked" or "Laughed" or "!!" would have been
nice. Instead, they read your message and did . . .

Nothing.

Not even the little flashing ellipsis bubble that shows
they are considering what you said.

Let Us . . . Trust

Truth time. Sometimes I feel ignored when I pray. It would be nice if, after every prayer, God would answer with an audible *ding!* or a thumbs-up emoji. I'd even be okay if the little ellipsis bubble stayed on my screen for a few minutes, so long as I knew God was working on my request.

I don't mind waiting for the answer if I'm sure someone out there is actually answering. But sometimes I feel nothing. Like I've been Holy-Ghosted.

Praying itself is, in one way, a huge step of faith. Think about it. You pour out your heart to a God you can't see. Why doesn't he at least acknowledge you? Why doesn't he do more to show you that he's there and that he's working on your request?

It's hard when we don't see our prayers moving the needle in real time. One thing the Bible assures us of, though is that God heard your prayer and is not ignoring it, even if you don't yet see how he's answering it. If Jesus is trustworthy at all, that must be true. And he proved his love for you at the cross. Jesus would not have died on a cross for us only to then ignore us. At the cross he demonstrated how far he would go to keep his promise never to leave or forsake us. The same God who kept the promise *then* has also promised to hear our prayers *now*.

The key to prayer, you see, is trust. Sometimes God doesn't do what you ask at all—not because he *doesn't* love you, but because he *does*.

Jesus made that point in one of the most delightful little conversations he ever had with his disciples. They asked, "Lord, teach us to pray" (Luke 11:1), and one of the truths he responded with was this: "What father among you, if his son asks for a fish, will instead of a fish give him a serpent; or if he asks for an egg, will give him a scorpion?" (verses 11–12).

Think through the logic here for a minute. Parents, if your children asked for chicken nuggets, would you say, "Okay, hold out your hands" before dropping cobras on them? No, of course not. (Though I do chuckle thinking of how my daughter would respond if I tossed a rubber snake into her hands after she asked for a Chick-fil-A five piece.) Truly, though, if it's mealtime and your child asks you for chicken nuggets, you'll probably get them some— and throw in a side of fries too. Parents love to make their children happy.

You may ask, "Then why hasn't God given me the 'nuggets' I asked for?" Well, reverse Jesus's illustration. Say your child asked for a scorpion to play with. Would you provide one? No way. You might offer a bunny, something that wouldn't torment your child. God does the same. God withholds from us some of what we ask for not in spite of his love for us, but *because* of his love for us.

Sometimes, I've heard it said, God shows his love for us by giving us what we *would* have asked for if we knew what he knew. Sometimes we ask for things we think are chicken nuggets but are actually scorpions. At some point in our lives, almost all of us learn to appreciate the words of that great theologian Garth Brooks who said that sometimes he thanks God for the unanswered prayers.

I'll be honest: I've prayed for bread and gotten something that looked like a scorpion. It stung and it hurt, but later on I appreciated how that sting set me on a path toward healing. I had to trust God through the pain, and only later would I learn how the sting of suffering became my bread of sustenance.

The cross itself looked and acted like a scorpion to the disciples, and they must have wondered if God was letting things get out of control. But that cross turned out to be God's instrument of salvation.

Never Give Up, Never Surrender

In the darkest days of World War II, Winston Churchill returned to his alma mater, the all-boys Harrow School. There, in an address to the school, he famously said the words: "This is the lesson: never give in, never give in, never, never, never, never."[34]

Jesus gave similar counsel to his disciples concerning prayer in Luke 18. The parable he told was about a widow

---

34. Winston Churchill, "Never Give In, Never, Never, Never, 1941," America's National Churchill Museum, accessed June 23, 2023, https://www.nationalchurchillmuseum.org/never-give-in-never -never-never.html.

who needed a judge to give her justice, but the judge ignored her because she didn't have enough money to hire a lawyer. (The lawyer was also a jerk who didn't really care about doing the right thing.) So this woman camped outside his house, and every time he went anywhere—to work, the grocery store, the gym—she pestered him about her need.

Now, watch this: "For a while he refused, but afterward he said to himself, 'Though I neither fear God nor respect man, yet because this widow keeps bothering me, I will give her justice, so that she will not beat me down by her continual coming'" (Luke 18:4–5). Then Jesus tells his disciples, *This is how you should pray to God.*

Jesus's point was not to compare himself to an unjust, crooked, cranky judge, but to contrast himself with one. He's saying that if even a spiteful judge will respond to persistent requests, how much more will a loving, heavenly Father respond to your persistent prayers?

Luke makes Jesus's point in the parable clear from the outset: "He told them a parable to the effect that they ought always to pray and not lose heart" (Luke 18:1).

You see, in contrast to this cranky ol' judge, we have a heavenly Father who loves to hear from us—who is so in touch with us that he knows when a hair falls from our heads, and who values us so much that he sent his Son to die for us. This parable teaches us that some blessings he only grants through persistence in asking.

Persistence is the practice of trust. Giving up says God can't or won't or doesn't care. Returning to God over and over shows that you know where the right answer will come from even if you haven't received it yet.

Here's a suggestion. When you pray, don't always start with the problem. Start your time with praise. Praise isn't buttering up God so he feels obligated to do what you asked after all those nice things you said about him. No, praise reminds you of the character of the God you are talking to. It gives you confidence in the request.

After all, God doesn't need to be reminded of your request, but you need to be reminded of his faithfulness. You're the one who needs the reminding, not him.

And yet, this parable makes it clear that God still wants you to bring the issue to him again and again, to the point that you feel rude. "No, really," Jesus says. "Keep asking." God only grants some requests through persistence.

"Why?" you ask. "If it's God's will to give it, why doesn't he do it the first time I ask?"

It's because persistence is one of the primary tools God uses to grow our faith. There's a form of exercise called resistance training, which increases muscle strength by forcing your muscles to work against your weight. Maybe you've seen people at the gym who are planking—resting on their elbows and toes while suspending their body in the air. It's tough, but *man*, the results are incredible. (I know from personal experience. As in, I've watched other people do it and seen how strong they get.)

Waiting for God's answer is spiritual planking. Your spirit grows stronger as it exerts its trust muscles. Every moment you don't quit, you reach new levels of faith and trust you never could have otherwise obtained. As the prophet Jeremiah put it, "The LORD is good to those who wait for him, to the soul who seeks him" (Lamentations 3:25). I don't particularly like waiting, but I've experienced its benefits multiple times now. Much of the best growth in my life has happened in periods when I was trying to be patient, unsure why God didn't seem to be answering my prayers.

More is happening than you think while you wait. God is doing a good work that only unveils over time. Embrace it by staying in the plank.

That'll Leave a Mark

Growing up, I loved wrestling. Not the wrestling at my high school—no one wants to see their friends wearing leotards, sweating and grunting in awkward positions. I mean *real* wrestling, with Hulk Hogan and the Undertaker and giant men with pretty hair smashing chairs over each other's backs. The kind of wrestling that's pronounced "rasslin'." Anytime someone climbs the turnbuckle (that's the fancy term for the corner of the ring), you know "a hurtin'" is about to happen.

There was actually a one-fall, winner-take-all, no-time-limit wrestling match in the Bible. It occurred in Genesis 32. In this corner, we have a devious deceiver named Jacob the Joker. In the other, a contender who's come all the way from heaven, weighing we're-not-sure-how-many pounds. An angel . . . or is he a man?

It's a wild story. Jacob, the grandson of Abraham, is in quite a pickle. His brother, Esau, is about to kill him (or so he thinks). This is the culmination of a thirty-year grudge. Which makes this, that's right . . . a grudge match. And to be honest, Jacob deserves it. He's been a real sleazebag.

Jacob hears that Esau is bringing a few friends to this grudge match—in fact, four hundred armed men. So he starts praying, as one does.

God responds by . . . *sending a man to wrestle with him*.

As if Jacob doesn't have enough problems with the four hundred men on their way, now he's got an angelic figure who wants to spar with him in the middle of the night.

They wrestle until dawn. I get tired just thinking about it.

The match looks like it's headed to a draw when the man/angel touches Jacob's hip and knocks it out of its socket. "Wait," you say. "If he had that kind of power all along, why didn't he pin Jacob in the first round?"

As Jacob lies there in pain, the "angel" asks him—*tells* him—"Say your name." Jacob says, "Jacob," which means "deceiver," at which point the angel shakes his head and says, "God has given you a new name. It's now Israel, which means, 'One who has struggled with God and prevailed.'"

I hope you never have to wrestle with a physical mani-festation of God during the midnight hours, but Jesus tells us we should expect our experience with God in prayer to sometimes feel like that. Some blessings, you see, come only through struggle—struggles that last through long nights of suffering. God uses that struggle to change or reshape our identity and produce in us a limp that compels us to depend on God.

The struggle leaves a mark, which is exactly how God intended it. Jacob's limp reminded him how much he needed God and how faithful God was. So will yours.

Remember: God is good to those who wait for him. God will put you through the wringer to soften your heart, strengthen your resolve, or remove that swagger in your step.

Dependence on him is his goal for you, and if dependence is the objective, then weakness becomes your advantage.

Read that last sentence again.

No, you don't have a prayer problem; you have a persistence problem. You jumped out of the fight too early because it hurt. Just when you were about to break through.

Real prayer almost always leaves us wounded, like Jacob—where God drives us to the end of ourselves, our abilities exhausted and our self-sufficiency shattered. From that point onward, we walk with a limp. Yes, we're weakened. But in more significant ways, God actually made us stronger. Beaten, bruised, and battle weary, but believing. God brings us to the point of despair, and we cling to him because we have no other alternative. With him, we're stronger than ever.

A List of Maybes

You won't always know why God isn't answering a prayer. Some things we won't fully understand until eternity. Sometimes the "delay" in the answer has nothing to do with your faith, your motives in asking, or anything about you that needs to change.

Let me give you a quick laundry list, however, of ways to check yourself if a prayer is not being answered. At some point or another, each of these is listed in the Bible as a possible reason for why a prayer is not being answered:

1. Maybe . . . You Are Not Pursuing His Will, but Yours

God will not pour blessing into your life when you are living in open rebellion to him. The Psalmist says, "If I had cherished iniquity in my heart, the Lord would not have listened" (Psalm 66:18). Peter says to husbands that if they are mistreating their wives, then their prayers will be hindered (1 Peter 3:7). Then add to that other places where Jesus says open sin cuts us off from the blessing of God. This applies to nonbelievers and believers. Is there unconfessed, willful sin in your life?

2. Maybe . . . God Has a Better Plan

We have to acknowledge, with our *limited* knowledge, that we can't know everything. As such, sometimes God overrules us—not out of spite, but out of love. We all do this for those we love. For instance, sometimes I overrule my kids' requests because I know better than them. Recently I needed to buy something for my sixteen-year-old to drive, and naturally, she wanted an Audi with gold rims. Instead I got her a Honda Accord with a stick shift. She said, "Why am I having to learn to drive a stick? This is so hard."

"I know," I said, "but (a) I think driving a stick is actually a valuable skill to have, (b) it keeps the car from being stolen, (c) it will help remove the temptation to have the phone in your hand when you drive, and (d) it means none of your friends will ever ask to borrow your car. That alone will make life easier." I gave her something different from what she asked for because I had a better plan, one that I believe will serve her better for a lifetime.

You can quibble with me over the wisdom of forcing her to learn to drive a stick shift. But you get the point: the wisdom of our heavenly Father is always better than ours.

Like we've said, sometimes God gives you what you would have asked for if you already knew what he knew.

3. Maybe . . . You Are Approaching God without Confidence in His Goodness

Jesus's half-brother, James, warns us about this when we pray: "If any of you lacks wisdom, let him ask God, who gives generously to all. . . . But let him ask in faith, with no doubting . . . For that person must not suppose that he will receive anything from the Lord" (James 1:5–7).

James says that when we approach God for help, we must ask "with no doubting." But he doesn't mean we should live at all times with absolute certainty about what God is doing and feel undisturbed peace. Every Christian I know struggles at times with doubt and confusion. He means we shouldn't approach God with divided loyalties, quietly pursuing a plan B if God doesn't come through.

On Sunday, you say, "God, I need you to work in my marriage." But on Monday, you are punishing your spouse or trying to manipulate or feeling justified in being unfaithful.

On Sunday, you say, "God, I need you to work in my finances." But on Monday you switch to plan B, which is to cheat on your taxes or overcharge your customers or stop giving your tithe.

Instead of this kind of double-mindedness, put all your confidence in him and surrender to doing things his way—no matter how long it takes for him to work out that goodness in your life.

4. Maybe . . . You Haven't Yet Prayed Long Enough

There may be a few more dark nights of wrestling ahead. Don't give up, friend. It could happen tomorrow or the next day. Pray with the expectation that God will answer. Hold on to God and say, like Jacob, "I will *not* let you go until you bless me."

I'm not sure how to explain this one, only to say that it is clear from Scripture that God gives some things only in response to persistence in prayer. Jesus told multiple parables reinforcing that truth, so don't give up. Many people, I'm convinced, stop praying in the eleventh hour when God planned to send the answer in the twelfth.

In his book *Release the Power of Prayer*, the nineteenth-century evangelist and orphanage founder George Müller tells the story of how he committed to pray for five individuals—friends of one of his sons—to be saved. [35] He resolved to pray for them every day until they became believers, and he prayed daily for eighteen months before the first one came to faith in Christ. (That's a long time! Have you ever prayed daily for the same thing for over five hundred days without seeing an answer?)

When that first friend was saved, George wrote in his journal that he praised God—but since there were four left, he would keep praying. After another five years, the second came to Christ. Müller kept praying. After six more years, the third one came to Christ. He kept praying. Thirty-six years later, George was an old man, and he wrote in his journal of those last two who were still unconverted: "I hope in God and I pray on and I look for the answer." It was fifty-two years after after George started praying that the final

---

35. "George Muller Persistent Prayer for 5 Individuals," Devotional, July 3, 2017, georgemueller.org/devotional/george-muller-persistent-prayer-for-5-individuals.

two were brought to faith in Christ—and that only after George's death.

Müller had taken seriously what Jesus wants to teach all his people: "they ought always to pray and not lose heart" (Luke 18:1).

In one of the most stirring scenes in Revelation, we see that God has not missed a single prayer we've ever prayed. "And the twenty-four elders fell down before the Lamb, each holding a harp, and golden bowls full of incense, which are the prayers of the saints" (Revelation 5:8).

For years and years and years, "saints" like you and me have prayed—for justice, for help—and sometimes it felt like we were being ignored. But God has heard every prayer we've prayed, and he kept them all.

I love how my fellow pastor Tyler Staton explains this passage: "Every prayer you've ever whispered, from the simplest throwaway request to the most heartfelt cry, God has collected it like a grandmother who scrapbooks a toddler's finger paints and scribbles. . . . God has treasured up every prayer we've ever uttered, even the ones we've forgotten, and he's still weaving their fulfillment, bending history in the direction of a great yes to you and me."[36]

One day, when God brings the final restoration to the earth, it will begin with him giving his final, categorical "yes" to all those prayers we prayed:

---

36. Tyler Staton, *Praying Like Monks, Living Like Fools* (Grand Rapids: Zondervan, 2022), 177.

> And another angel came and stood at the altar with a golden censer, and he was given much incense to offer with the prayers of all the saints on the golden altar before the throne, and the smoke of the incense, with the prayers of the saints, rose before God from the hand of the angel. Then the angel took the censer and filled it with fire from the altar and threw it on the earth, and there were peals of thunder, rumblings, flashes of lightning, and an earthquake. (Revelation 8:3–5)

Think about it: right now in heaven there are golden bowls brimming with our cries for healing and justice and restoration and vindication. Some of them are prayers I have prayed. Sometimes God answers our prayers for healing, justice, or restoration now. But sometimes, he delays—and we pray for thirty or forty years before getting an answer. Sometimes we die without receiving the answer. But that doesn't mean he ignored us. Rest assured, as the writer of Revelation shows us, he's kept every one.

In fact, the final restoration of the earth begins with God giving a categorical and unequivocal yes to all those prayers that we and other saints have prayed over the years. All the justice and healing and restoration and vindication that we yearned for will, in that moment, be fully and finally given to us.

In the end, every prayer of a believer is an answered prayer. Never, never, never, never give up. Pray persistently.

The Lord Is My Shepherd . . . and He Is Enough

If you're asking about unanswered prayer, I'm going to guess you're currently experiencing something painful. Something like . . .

- A disobedient child running in the wrong direction
- The loss of a loved one
- Betrayal by family or friends
- Infertility
- An addiction you can't seem to shake
- Chronic pain
- Frustration over a job, a ministry, or living conditions

Of course, I could go on. But the point is, if you're asking about unanswered prayer, there's likely something you want to experience *now* that God wants you to wait for. And while you wait, you need confidence. So I want to turn our attention to Psalm 23. I know, it's normally read during funerals, but if you're struggling right now, you're mourning the loss of something. You need hope. Use Psalm 23 to remind yourself that you have all you need.

The Lord is my shepherd; I shall not want.

Since I have the Lord and he's watching over me, I have everything I need. I really don't need anything to change because the Lord is on my side.

He makes me lie down in green pastures.

What do sheep usually do in a green pasture? They eat. If David is lying down in a green pasture, it means he is so "full" of the Shepherd's presence he doesn't even feel hungry anymore. A nap is the ultimate act of comfort, and he is safe.

He leads me beside still waters.

God takes me where I find satisfaction, in peaceful places with plenty.

He restores my soul.

My heart and my will were broken, shaken, and disappointed, but God fills me and restores me, putting me back on my feet. With his presence beside me and his promises before me, I can keep going.

He leads me in paths of righteousness for his name's sake.

He guides me to new places, new challenges, and new adventures. Sometimes I don't like it, but I always find that where God guides, he provides.

Even though I walk through the valley of the shadow of death.

My path is not without its share of dark days and even darker nights. Because God is with me, however, I have no reason to be afraid. Night is always like day to him. He is my sun and my shield. He sees through the shadows. I am not alone.

I will fear no evil, for you are with me; your rod and your staff, they comfort me.

He stands over me, ready with the instruments of direction and protection.

You prepare a table before me in the presence of my enemies.

Eating is a sign of rest and fulfillment. I feast on his presence and rest in his protection in the midst of darkness and chaos.

You anoint my head with oil; my cup overflows.

Anointing is a blessing, an assurance that God's Spirit is with me, covering me from head to toe. The blessings that God gives me, even in pain, are so abundant that they overflow.

Surely goodness and mercy shall follow me all the days of my life.

I can't escape goodness and mercy. They are always right behind me. As Christians, we love to talk about the importance of following Jesus. It's just as important to recognize, however, that he is following us, turning our tragedy into triumph and our misery into miracle.

And I shall dwell in the house of the LORD forever.

Not only is God with me now, but he will be forever. There is nowhere I can go outside the scope of his control, and nothing I can do would put me outside the scope of his love. No one can threaten me, harm me, or separate me from his love.

To all of you who are unhappy, anxious, or afraid because your prayers aren't being answered . . .

Look up. Your Shepherd has never left you.

The path of righteousness is not so much a lifestyle as it is the confidence that all you need is Jesus. As David shows us: If you've got the Shepherd, you've got enough. Knowing him, trusting him, treasuring him, being able to rest in his presence—that is the greatest thing God can teach you while you wait.

He has not ignored your prayer request; he's answering needs you didn't even know you had.

Stop Focusing on the Problem and Focus on the Promise

I saw somewhere recently that experts believe we have between six thousand and seven thousand thoughts per day. When I looked this up, I then found *other* experts who say we have between seventy thousand and eighty thousand thoughts per day. The difference between the two is determined by how much coffee you drink.

OK, I made up that last part. I don't know which "experts" are right, but one thing we can all agree on? Our minds do a lot of work during the day. We think *a lot* of thoughts.

How many of those thoughts are rooted in one of God's promises? Did you know the Bible contains more than three thousand promises? Here are just a few of them:

1. God has a good plan for you—to bless you and make you a blessing (Jeremiah 29:11).

2. God will give you rest (Matthew 11:28).

3. God will give you strength equal to the task he assigns (Philippians 4:13).

4. God will provide your daily bread (Matthew 6:11).

5. Nothing will separate you from God's love (Romans 8:38–39).

6. He bears your burdens and fights for you (Joshua 23:10).

7. He delights to give you the kingdom (Matthew 16:19).

8. The Spirit prays for you about things you don't know how to pray for yourself (Romans 8:26).

9. He will never leave or forsake you (Joshua 1:5).

10. He will supply all your need according to his riches in Christ Jesus (Philippians 4:19).

That's ten. Only 2,990 to go. Even if those were the only ten promises, I'd be feeling pretty good. No wonder David exclaims, "How precious to me are your thoughts, O God! How vast is the sum of them! If I would count them, they are more than the sand" (Psalm 139:17–18).

So why is it that when we're faced with a problem, we dedicate 5,789 worries to the problem and none (or very few) to the promises of God?

Your confidence, security, and joy in life will be in direct proportion to your awareness of the promises of God. Saturate yourself in them. Meditate on them. Memorize them. As Moses said, "They are not just idle words for you—they are your life" (Deuteronomy 32:47 NIV).

Promises are God's pre-answers to your prayers, so trust in them. Resting in the promises of God not only brings peace to your soul, but also connects you to the power God is ready to give.

And whatever you do, don't give up, don't lose heart. God never does. He's listening right now.

Let me end this chapter by sharing something God recently did that demonstrates his wonderful, surprising faithfulness in answering prayer.

Picture this: in Winston-Salem, North Carolina, I'm standing on the stage of a church we planted. This church is experiencing what I can only describe as revival, and as I look out over the audience, packed to the gills with standing room only, the Holy Spirit reminds me of prayers I prayed *over thirty years ago* when I was in my teens.

You see, I grew up in Winston-Salem, and the church I grew up in was a fairly standard, not very exciting Baptist church. I had gotten saved at sixteen (the best of my four baptisms) and really wanted my church to experience revival—the kind I'd read about where people came to Christ by the hundreds and the sense of God's presence became palpable. My best friend and I showed up every Sunday an hour and a half before church to pray in the sanctuary for God to pour out that revival.

We prayed faithfully for a year, and every single Sunday, I thought, *This just might be the week. The time might just be now. Maybe today God is going to open up heaven.* And every week, I left bitterly disappointed because the church services remained as dead as they always were.

Eventually, I went off to college, got busy, and started to focus on other things. It always remained a curiosity to me, however, why God did not answer that prayer. It seemed so obvious that he would *want* revival there. This was a prayer squarely in the center of God's will, it seemed. Why was he not listening to me? I was a new Christian praying with childlike faith.

Fast-forward to the present day. There I am, standing in front of this incredible new church. You can stand on the front porch of this church and actually see my old church way up on the hill. A lot of the younger people I grew up with have come to this new church plant, and this congregation is experiencing a genuine outpouring of revival.

Hundreds of people have come to Christ. As I stand there, the Holy Spirit overwhelms me with these words: "You thought I wasn't listening to you thirty years ago, but I was. *I heard every word.* I just answered it differently—and better—than you expected."

I believe the day will come when we will experience answers like that to every prayer we've ever prayed in faith.

Whatever you're going through, I can assure you, *God is listening*.

So never give up.

7

How Can I Know God's Will for My Life?

The Magic 8 Ball was a novelty toy invented way back in 1950. Albert Carter and Abe Bookman developed a round toy they called the Crystal Ball, which held a dark blue liquid and a floating die inside. For Carter, it seemed, the "toy" was more than a novelty. His mother considered herself a clairvoyant who communicated with ghosts (including Sir Arthur Conan Doyle, author of the Sherlock Holmes mysteries). For Carter, this little crystal ball was a way of soliciting supernatural help when making decisions.

It was a flop.

A flop, that is, until they found a partner in Brunswick Billiards. Together they revamped the idea and created the Magic 8 Ball, which has been bought by millions of Americans and has probably determined more destinies than we can imagine—including what colleges to attend, proposals to accept, and jobs to take.

You ask a question, then shake the Magic 8 Ball, and it answers: "Signs point to yes," "Outlook not so good," or "Reply hazy, try again."

My guess is that not many readers of this book carry around a Magic 8 Ball to consult during decisions. (And if you do—hey, this is a safe space. I appreciate your honesty.) But just about everyone I know wants help to figure out the best way to make decisions, which is probably why "How can I know God's will for my life?" might be the question I get asked more than any other.

People always want to know if God gives them "signs" about the decisions they should make, and if so, how they can discern those signs. The question sometimes sounds like this:

"Pastor, I've been praying to God about asking this girl out . . . and then on the way home from work the other day I saw a billboard, and the name of the company on the sign started with the same first letter as the girl's name. *And* the color of the font on the billboard was the same as the color of her eyes, and the last two digits of the listed phone number were the same as her age. How could this all be a coincidence? Pastor, I just *know* it's God telling me to ask her out!"

Maybe. But, well, probably not. Sounds to me more like the prologue to a restraining order.

Others say God lets them know they've discovered his will for their life through an unexplained warm feeling, goosebumps, a cloud formation, or what a friend of mine calls "liver shivers." To be clear, I don't want to downplay the mysterious leadership of the Spirit. Sometimes God really *does* do miraculous things to get our attention.

More often than not, however, lurking behind these tendencies of ours is an assumption that God is playing a game of divine peekaboo—as if his will for us is hidden behind one of three secret doors, and we have to guess which one is right without any real clues or help.

But is that how God wants us thinking of his will for our lives? In the words of the Magic 8 Ball, "My sources say no."

No Five Easy Steps

Let's set the stage here a bit. (Historical context always helps.) Up until fifty years ago, there was almost no talk about knowing the will of God—at least not in terms of personal decision-making. Looking through the sermons of the early church and the Reformation, I could not find a single one on this topic. Let that sink in.

For two thousand years people have studied the Bible as much (if not more) than we do, yet this question did not surface as a top three, a top ten, or even a top one hundred. Now it's our main question.

Hmm. What does that mean? Maybe it reveals that we've become a "selfie" culture, defined by individualism, and we now think of the will of God as an important tool in achieving our self-actualization.

This isn't always the case, but I've seen it happen more times than I can count: well-intended believers turn the will of God into an idol. I say that because they seem to want to know the will of God more than God himself. It's almost as if discerning the will of God becomes a substitute for trusting God—a way to remove all uncertainty from our lives and guarantee success.

And by "we," I really mean "we." I find myself doing the exact same thing.

We all want Five Easy Steps to Finding the Will of God for My Life—God's Will for Dummies—but it just doesn't work that way. We want a quick fix. "Just shoot me straight, God! Should I major in business or religion? Should I break up with Madison or ask her to marry me? Should I move to Boston or Chicago?"

It's not that God doesn't care about any of that. He does. But in Scripture, God's will is much more about the *who* than the *what*—when you *become* the will of God, you'll *do* the will of God.

It might help here to understand a little more about the phrase "God's will." One time in college I looked up every reference to the will of God and found Scripture presenting the concept at least three different ways.

1. God's Providential Will

This refers to the mysterious way God controls history and works events toward his purposes. For example, Jesus was going to the cross to die for our sins. Nothing could stop that from happening. In Ephesians 1:11, Paul says that God "works all things according to the counsel of his will." He simply means that God guides all of history toward his ends, and not one thing he wants done will be left undone. As we saw in chapter four, not one strand of history is out of place. Knowing about God's providential will is supposed to fill us with peace, since we know God is ruling and reigning. And no matter how out of control life seems, we can remember that nothing is outside of God's control.

2. God's Moral Will

This refers to God's commands. In 1 Thessalonians 4:3 Paul says that God's will is our "sanctification." He wants us to grow in holiness. He doesn't want us to kill others, commit adultery, or steal. He *does* want us to love one another, care for the poor, worship him, and follow him in his mission. Unlike God's providential will, this is one where we can deviate from his plan (to our detriment, of course). When you see the phrase "the will of God" in Scripture (and it does not appear that often), it is usually referring to God's moral will.

3. God's Guidance in Nonmoral Decisions

This is usually what people today mean when they ask about God's will for their lives. They're seeking God's direction over what job to take, what city to move to, what church to attend, or what guy to marry. Maybe they ask God what shirt to wear today, what to bring for lunch, and what route to drive to work. That's great. He loves us and wants to be in all the nooks and crannies of our lives. But he also may not give the same clarity here that he does in the second category (His moral will).

The Bible speaks clearly on categories one and two. They are nonnegotiable. But the last one trips up a lot of people, since they believe that if they choose Door #1 instead of Door #2, then their lives will be ruined. They worry that God had so many good things for them . . . but because they went to Charleston instead of Atlanta, they never ran into the guy who recommended them for that dream job, or never met the woman who would mother their children.

But here's the thing: God knew you were going to choose Charleston. It may be a surprise to you, but it wasn't to him. Your nonmoral decisions aren't going to accidentally put you on God's Plan B (or Plan C or Plan D) path for your life. It just doesn't work that way.

And yet, people toss and turn, chewing their nails and sobbing in their small group, convinced that God has some specific plan for them . . . *but they missed it*. Exhausting.

My advice to them often seems counterintuitive: *you're obsessing over the wrong thing*.

Obsess Over the Right Things

If you really want to know the will of God, stop obsessing over the wrong things and start obsessing over the right ones.

"And what are those?" you ask.

1. Obsess over Knowing God and Becoming Like Him

Remember how I said that following the will of God is more about *who* than *what*? To the degree to which you know God and walk as Jesus walked, *you are fulfilling the will of God*. God desires for you to become like him. That's what maturity is—learning to think as God thinks.

My wife and I trained our children to grow up and think like adults should think. When they were little, their lives were governed by a ton of rules. But the more they grew, the less we dictated to them. Our hope was that they would not need rules for every minute of their lives; instead, they would *become* people who would make grown-up decisions on their own. We didn't want them to ask us for direction every time they encountered a fork in the road. Our goal has always been to lead them to maturity, helping them navigate situations we haven't even imagined yet.

In the same way, Christian maturity isn't best expressed by asking God to supernaturally reveal every decision you should ever make. Christian maturity is learning to think like God thinks.

Remember the WWJD bracelets from the nineties? WWJD stood for "What would Jesus do?" Those things were *everywhere*. I tried to convince a couple of my friends that the letters stood for "Women Want J. D." Fortunately, that never caught on. Those bracelets aren't nearly as popular now, though I still see them from time to time. Regardless, it's a worthwhile question. Wherever you are, whatever you're doing, you can and should ask, "What would Jesus do if he were in this situation?"

And here's the thing: you might instinctively know the answer *because you already know Jesus so well*. Because you know his Word. Because you spend time with him. Because you're actively following his moral will. As you "become the will of God," you instinctively start doing the will of God.

I'd go so far as to say that you will not know the will of God any more than you are conformed to the character of God, and you won't be conformed to the character of God any more than you know the Word of God. So if you tell me you are seeking his will but you're not studying his Word, I'd say you probably understand neither his will nor his Word.

2. Quit Obsessing about the Details of Individual Decisions

God expects us to make the most of our decisions using the "natural" faculties he has given us. Study Scripture to see if it says anything specific about your situation. Consider all the facts—make a T-chart of positives and negatives.

Seek counsel from others who can often see things you don't. Proverbs says that in a multitude of counselors there is safety and victory (Proverbs 11:14), and throughout Acts we see God guiding the apostles by means of other members in the church.

Take time to consider what God has done in your life previously. Maybe you'll see a pattern he's been developing. You might see how he's been preparing you for an opportunity, a door he's just opened.

Slow down and give God time to work. And, of course, saturate the whole process in prayer, trusting that if you need more information, God will supply it.

And then, when it's time to make the decision, make it boldly, without hesitation. Trust that if you make the wrong decision, God your Shepherd will gently override you and lead you into the right pasture.

Listen, I have good news: God lost faith in your decision-making abilities back in the garden of Eden. There he determined that if you were going to get where he wanted you to go, it wouldn't be because of your wise choices but because of his compassionate guidance.

Following God's guidance is supposed to be a mostly stress-free experience. Proverbs 3:6 promises us, after all, that if in all our ways we acknowledge God, he will direct our paths.

My student pastor once told me to draw a wall between the two clauses in that verse—between "in all your ways acknowledge him" and "he shall direct your paths." He told me the wall represented the division between my side of the verse and God's side. My part of the agreement is to acknowledge him, which means obeying everything I know to obey and availing myself of every resource he's provided to help me make the decision.

His side of the wall is to make my paths straight (Proverbs 3:6 NIV). "You do your part," the pastor said, "and God will do his part. Most of the stress in your life will come from you getting on God's side of the wall. In a panic you may say, 'But what about this outcome?' or, 'What happens if I get this wrong?' But God very patiently says, 'Get back over there on your side of the wall.'" That advice has served as a lifeline in some of the most major decisions of my life, and a little sketch of a wall remains there in my Bible, between the two clauses of Proverbs 3:6, to this day.

Sure, a burning bush or Damascus Road experience would be great. But rather than waiting for a voice from the sky to tell us which way to go, Proverbs 3:6 tells us to *just get moving* in obedience to what we already know. As we serve and obey God in the things he has revealed in his Word, he promises to guide us to where he wants us to go.

In other words, you will discover the parts of the will of God that you *don't* know as you obey the parts you *do* know. God steers moving ships, so get involved at your church. Start using your spiritual gifts. Go on short-term mission trips. Join a small group. Shoot, *start* a small group. Find an organization helping people in your community and join it.

I promise that as you execute his commands, you will discover who you were meant to be. And as you *become* the will of God, you'll *do* the will of God.

God's Calling as the Intersection of Three Circles

I believe that we can discern God's call on our lives by considering the intersection of three circles: ability, affinity, and affirmation.[37]

Ability refers to what you're good at.

Affinity refers to what you are passionate about. Where do you really feel alive, like you are doing what you were created to do, with a sense of God's pleasure in you as you do it? (Note: you will not be good at everything you are passionate about. I am passionate, for example, about worship music. But I can't play any instruments and I'm not a gifted singer. So, passionate though I may be, becoming a full-time worship leader, songwriter, or recording artist is probably not God's calling on my life. Our worship pastor has awkwardly made that clear to me multiple times.)

Affirmation refers to those places where others in the church affirm God is using you in their lives. Honestly, this might be the most important of the three *A*'s. Early on in my preaching, for example, several people told me that when I opened God's word, God spoke to them through

37. I credit pastor and author Tim Keller with this general idea, although see Keller's original tweet for some variation: https://twitter.com/timkellernyc/status/1468597238444314624?lang=en.

me. Affirmation by the body of Christ gave me real clarity about what God had gifted me to do.

Generally speaking, you'll discover your calling at the intersection of those three circles. If you're good at something, and you love to do it, and others affirm that God's hand is on you while you are doing it, then there's a good chance God wants to use you in that way for his kingdom.

Is that calling always experienced as vocational ministry? Nope. As we saw in chapter three, God calls and equips many people to go into (so-called) secular work. In fact, the first time the phrase "filled with the Spirit" is used in the Bible, it refers to two guys, Bezalel and Oholiab, who were filled by God's spirit for a *secular* task—namely, artistry and craftsmanship (Exodus 31:1–6). Whatever you do in the world, you should do it at God's direction, empowered by his Spirit—which means wherever you go in the world, you can turn that place into a ministry.

Above all, grow your relationship with God so you become the kind of person God promises to guide. Remember, the will of God is less something you do and more something you become. When you "become" the will of God, you'll do the will of God instinctively.

Be the Sheep

I'm revisiting this section from my book *Just Ask*, which was published in 2021. I think it perfectly sums up how to pray the will of God into your life. I use this method all the time in decisions I make, both big and small.

I call it the "sheep prayer" because in this situation, I see myself as the sheep needing guidance from the Shepherd. The prayer centers on this important premise—I'm an idiot. Compared to the Shepherd, I know nothing. Like a sheep, I find myself stuck, defenseless, and, many times, upside down and unable to get back on my feet.

What do I do? I call out to my omni-Shepherd, who can see it all, knows it all, and understands it all.

Here's how the "sheep prayer" comes out for me:

"Lord, I have this decision to make, and I have done my best to listen to you and figure out the best option. I've sought out good counsel, and I've prayed about it and now, God, this is what I think I am going to do. But, God, I know I am a sheep, and sheep are idiots. Thus, I have no confidence in my ability to make this decision. But I do have confidence in your competence and compassion as my Good Shepherd to guide me. So, if this is not the right decision, I'm asking you to take your rod and your staff and move me into whatever path you want me on."

This is a humbling thing to pray, but an empowering way to live. We don't need to lean on ourselves and figure it out for ourselves and then spend life worrying that we may have got it wrong. We lean on him, follow him, and spend life knowing he has us right where he wants us to be. Even our own mistakes, and even other people's wrongdoing, cannot prevent him from guiding us in paths of righteousness (Psalm 23:3).

If you entrust yourself to him, he won't let you mess it up, nor will he let others mess it up. No one messes with our Shepherd's sheep! He laid down his life for them. Think about it: at this point, he has more invested in your life than you do—God spilled the blood of his own son to save you. He won't neglect his investment.

In the end, it really is that simple: *Be the sheep and trust the Shepherd.*

The Bible does talk about God's guidance in our lives, but it puts the em-PHA-sis on different syl-LAB-les than we typically do—namely, on knowing the ways of God and becoming the kind of person God wants you to be. As you do that, God promises to guide you in the execution of his specific will for your life.

So the best and most relevant question isn't *what* but *who*—not "What is God's will for my life?" but "Who does God guide?"

A humble, trusting, obedient sheep, that's who.

Embrace the freedom of a sheep. Well-cared-for sheep get to where they need to be not because they are super capable as sheep but because they have an amazing shepherd. And you have the most amazing Shepherd of them all.

8

I Believe in God.
Why Do I Still Struggle
with Anxiety?

I wanted to start this section with a list of things people are most anxious about. But as I perused the surveys available online about what worries most people, I found myself worrying about a bunch of stuff I hadn't thought about in years. And then I was worried about why I hadn't been worried. Then I was worried that I *was* worried about what I wasn't previously worried about. It was a mess.

I'm sure you have your own list of things you are worried about. And I'm sure it's longer than you want to get into.

Worry often hums in the background of life. A friend of mine says anxiety functions like an ominous soundtrack that colors the mood of every moment of every day. It's kind of like when you're watching a movie and the foreboding music starts to swell in the background. You don't see anything going wrong yet; the teenage boy is riding his bike peacefully in the woods. But the music makes you suspect something bad is about to happen.

Many of us live our whole lives with that feeling. We don't even know what exactly we're worried about, but the droning hum of anxiety convinces us something terrible is on the way.

My job here is to show you, biblically, how to handle the sources of your worry.

Let's Start with the Command

I always find it helpful to start by reflecting on a direct command from Scripture *not* to worry. Paul says it plainly: "Do not be anxious about anything" (Philippians 4:6). If you're prone to worry, that might not feel tremendously encouraging. *Thanks, Paul, for the command. I'm all good now.*

But here's the thing: God wouldn't command us to do something unless he had made all provisions necessary for us to obey that command. It would be cruel to tell your children not to worry about what they will eat for lunch if you have no money to buy lunch or no idea where to get food. We tell our kids not to worry about lunch *because we have it covered.* That's why God tells us not to worry too. He can and will handle whatever we're worried about.

So I actually like starting there. That verse is as much a promise as it is a command—or, rather, a command that grows out of a promise. If God invites us to live free from worry, *that kind of life is actually possible.*

The question is . . . how?

Before we start, let me give a disclaimer. Throughout this chapter I'll sometimes use the words *worry* and *anxiety* interchangeably, but I understand that counselors and psychologists use them differently.

Worry refers to temporary stress focused more on day-to-day operations (such as food, money, rent, tests, or doctors). Worry comes from being overly concerned about something in your life.

Anxiety is a deeper, more stressful reaction to situations that you believe pose a substantive threat to you or your loved ones. It's an ongoing, tense soundtrack that hums in the background of your life.

The lessons we learn here are applicable to both situations. Both, you see, have similar root causes. We live in a stressful world, and the recent data collected about anxiety is, well, a bit worrisome. The Anxiety and Depression Association of America (which sounds like a fun place to work) has released these statistics:

- In the United States "anxiety disorders are the most common mental health concern." They affect over forty million adults, which is 19.1 percent of the US population.[38]

---

38. "Anxiety Disorders," National Alliance on Mental Illness, reviewed December 2017, https://www.nami.org/About-Mental-Illness/Mental-Health-Conditions/Anxiety-Disorders.

- Ninety-one percent of Gen Z report significant psychological symptoms due to stress and anxiety.[39] A CDC report shows that teen girls who would say they are "persistently sad and hopeless" has grown from 36 percent to 57 percent since 2011.[40]
- Nearly 32 percent of young people between thirteen and eighteen are affected by anxiety disorders.[41]
- The World Health Organization reported that anxiety and depression increased 25 percent as a result of the pandemic.[42]

Anxiety, depression, and other mood disorders can have root causes as varied as our genetics, families of origin, family histories, chemical imbalances, diets, past trauma, and spiritual issues.

---

39. Sophie Bethune, "Gen Z more likely to report mental health concerns," *Monitor on Psychology* 50, no. 1 (January 2019), https://www.apa.org/monitor/2019/01/gen-z.

40. "CDC report shows concerning increases in sadness and exposure to violence among teen girls and LGBQ+ youth," Centers for Disease Control and Prevention, March 9, 2023, https://www.cdc.gov/nchhstp/newsroom/fact-sheets/healthy-youth/sadness-and-violence-among-teen-girls-and-LGBQ-youth-factsheet.html.

41. "Any Anxiety Disorder," National Institute of Mental Health, accessed June 23, 2023, https://www.nimh.nih.gov/health/statistics/any-anxiety-disorder.

42. "COVID-19 pandemic triggers 25% increase in prevalence of anxiety and depression worldwide," World Health Organization, March 2, 2022, https://www.who.int/news/item/02-03-2022-covid-19-pandemic-triggers-25-increase-in-prevalence-of-anxiety-and-depression-worldwide.

In this chapter, I am focusing primarily on the spiritual causes—because, well, I'm a pastor, and that's what I know best. But not only that: much of our anxiety contains at least *some* spiritual dimension. That's not to say there are no other legitimate factors contributing to your anxiety. It's usually a mix.

In other words, I'm not suggesting that you read this chapter *instead* of going to see your psychologist or your doctor. I would suggest you read this chapter *alongside* your treatment. Often, we ignore the spiritual dimensions of our anxiety, and we try to fix everything with a pill, change of schedule, or some breathing techniques. Our bodies, souls, spirits, emotions, thoughts, and past memories are all intrinsically connected, and quite often, our anxiety is rooted in all of them.

You can think about disruptive surface emotions (sadness, anxiety, fear, etc.) like smoke. If you follow the trail of smoke, you will eventually find the fire causing it. That's your *real* problem. Firefighters don't try to "fix the smoke"; they address the fire itself. The smoke isn't the problem; it's the evidence of the problem. If you follow the smoke of your emotions *down*, you discover what's on fire in your life, deep in your soul. You may even find that the smoke is coming from an altar you've erected in pursuit of a false god.

So think of anxiety like smoke. We must follow that smoke to the fire before it spreads throughout the whole house of our lives.

Today's Provisions and Tomorrow's God

Let's look at what Jesus says about worry in what I believe
to be one of his most profound and insightful teachings.
It comes at the end of Matthew 6, right in the middle of
his famous Sermon on the Mount, and I constantly direct
people to this passage amid counseling. Here's the beautiful
message in its entirety.

> Therefore I tell you, do not be anxious about your
> life [there's that command again!], what you will
> eat or what you will drink, nor about your body,
> what you will put on. Is not life more than food,
> and the body more than clothing? Look at the birds
> of the air: they neither sow nor reap nor gather into
> barns, and yet your heavenly Father feeds them. Are
> you not of more value than they? And which of you
> by being anxious can add a single hour to his span
> of life? And why are you anxious about clothing?
> Consider the lilies of the field, how they grow: they
> neither toil nor spin, yet I tell you, even Solomon in
> all his glory was not arrayed like one of these. But
> if God so clothes the grass of the field, which today
> is alive and tomorrow is thrown into the oven, will
> he not much more clothe you, O you of little faith?
> Therefore do not be anxious, saying, "What shall we
> eat?" or "What shall we drink?" or "What shall we
> wear?" For the Gentiles seek after all these things,
> and your heavenly Father knows that you need

them all. But seek first the kingdom of God and his
righteousness, and all these things will be added to
you. Therefore do not be anxious about tomorrow,
for tomorrow will be anxious for itself. Sufficient for
the day is its own trouble. (Matthew 6:25–34)

In this passage, Jesus makes three main points about anxiety.

1. Anxiety Minimizes God (Matthew 25–33)

Most of us think of anxiety as an emotion that naturally
arises from the uncertainty of life, but that thinking comes
from bad theology.

We worry most about what we are devoted to the most.
*Whatever you see as the most important elements in your life,
you will worry about.*

Let me prove that. I don't worry that much about *your*
kids' grades. I mean, I care about your kids in a theoretical
sense, and I want them to do well, but the fact that they
failed another math test doesn't personally keep me up at
night. (And before you get offended, I'd bet you've never lost
a night of sleep over my kids' problems either.) I'm just not
that devoted to them. Neither does my blood pressure go
up imagining what your boss thinks about that project you
turned in last week. If you ask me to pray about it, I will, but
I'll likely forget about it after a couple of days.

We choose to worry about what we are most devoted
to, which is why Jesus started this discussion on anxiety by

challenging us to consider what we regard as *sine qua non* or essential qualities of life.[43]

See the word *therefore* in Matthew 6:25? "Therefore I tell you, do not be anxious about your life, what you will eat or what you will drink, nor about your body, what you will put on."

You've heard it before: Anytime you see the word *therefore* in the Bible, look and see what it's "there for," because it's connecting what is about to be said with what has just been said. In this case, the "therefore" of verse 25 connects us to the big point Jesus made in verse 24: "No one can serve two masters, for either he will hate the one and love the other, or he will be devoted to the one and despise the other. You cannot serve God and money."

Jesus knows that many of us regard money as the most essential element for making life work, so when it's time to discuss anxiety, he starts with our bank accounts. He's basically saying, "If you are devoted to money, then that's what you'll worry about all the time." He's right. If you think money is the one indispensable ingredient for a good life (like most of us do), then you will worry all the time about it—getting it, keeping it, and not losing it.

Then he asks a series of questions that challenge our devotion to money. He asks in verse 25: "Is not life more than food, and the body more than clothing?"

---

43. Andy Stanley, "Devotion Emotion" (sermon), part 1 of the *Why Worry?* series, North Point Community Church.

Hmm. Okay, good question. Well, I kind of like food and clothing. It's hard to imagine a good life without those things. Jesus then gives two examples showing creatures in God's Kingdom who don't worry at all about food and clothing yet are amply endowed with both.

- First, he tells us to consider the birds (verse 26): "Look at the birds of the air: they neither sow nor reap nor gather into barns, and yet your heavenly Father feeds them." Birds don't spend much time worrying about savings, yet they never seem to lack because God takes care of them.

- Second, he says to check out the wildflowers (verses 28–29): "Consider the lilies of the field, how they grow: they neither toil nor spin, yet I tell you, even Solomon in all his glory was not arrayed like one of these." Flowers don't spend much time worrying about looking pretty, yet they are beautiful because God adorns them.

The point is not that we shouldn't save, or that we shouldn't ever use money to buy nice things for ourselves. (We aren't birds or flowers, after all.) It's just that we should not be focused on money as our primary source of security and beauty because our heavenly Father is a better source and guarantee of those things.

The key point comes in verse 32, when Jesus says, "It's the people who don't know God who worry about all these things. You have a Heavenly Father who knows what you need" (paraphrased). He knows we need food and clothes. And we know he loves us, so we trust in him to provide all we need of both, just like he does for birds and flowers.

I was once asked by a sincere Christian teenager who struggled with anxiety concerning what others thought about her, "If I'm really spiritual, will I just not care if people like me or if I don't have friends?"

I told her, "No, you will still care. God created you with a desire for friendship and a desire to be loved and accepted by others. Jesus's point is not that knowing him makes these things irrelevant to you, but that you can rest assured that you have a Heavenly Father who knows you need them. Can't you trust him? After all, look at the security he gives to the birds and the beauty he gives to the flowers. We know he cares more for us, his children, than for them. After all, he died for you and not for birds and flowers. If God takes such good care of the flowers, won't he take care of you, too, and supply the friends you need?"

If you are going to fixate on something, fixate on God. And when you do, "all these things" will be added to you (verse 33). What are the "all these things" Jesus refers to? Things like food. Beauty. Significance. Friends. Safety. Jesus didn't say, "Put me first and all these things will become irrelevant to you." He created you with a need for them.

If I had to choose a life verse, it would be that one, Matthew 6:33. Honestly, I can't hear that promise enough. Jesus tells us that if we want to worry, then we should worry about pleasing God and doing his will. Focus primarily on obeying him, and he will take care of everything else—including our relationships, financial security, what we're going to wear, where we're going to live, what kind of impact our life makes, and all other necessities. If we absolutely must worry, let's worry about keeping ourselves close to God.

Show Me the Money

Let me offer one additional encouragement here about money, since that is what most people worry about most.

When it comes to worrying about money, people tend to fall into one of two personality types—savers and spenders. Some people, if they get an extra $500 in their paycheck, want to rush out and buy a new TV. Those are the spenders. The savers want to save that $500 for a rainy day. Thanks to God's sense of humor, these two different personalities often marry each other, and both think the other one has a problem with money.

The saver thinks the spender is foolish and impulsive; the spender thinks the saver is miserly and fearful. In truth, though, *both* can have a problem with money if they are looking to money to provide something only God can provide. Savers look to money to provide security, while spenders look to money to provide significance. Savers find joy in the future. Spenders find joy in the right now.

Jesus addressed both individually in his illustration. Birds don't hoard food, yet God keeps them secure. Flowers don't spend money on petals, yet God crowns them with beauty and significance.

Jesus is saying: stop worrying about money and focus on keeping yourself in fellowship with God. Make him your primary source of security and joy. And when you do, he'll take care of you better than he does the birds and the flowers.

C. S. Lewis had a great way of summarizing this. I'll paraphrase, but essentially, he said that in life, there are first things (God) and second things (everything else like food, companionship, finances, friendship, etc.). If you put first things first, God promises to take care of second things. But when you put second things first, not only will you lose the first things, but you'll also lose your ability to enjoy the second things.[44]

That's C. S. Lewis's spin on Matthew 6:33, and it's a good one.

Of course, you can apply this principle beyond financial worries—to other concerns such as parenting, medical issues, marriage, education, and work. Remember, seeking first the kingdom of God doesn't mean you never think about these other things; it just means you don't believe your security, stability, freedom, or joy are contingent upon them. As Jesus said, no man can serve two masters.

Jesus used the word *cares* when talking about "the cares of this world." The word has been interpreted by Bible scholars

---

44. "Reflections: First and Second Things," C. S. Lewis Institute, July 1, 2017, https://www.cslewisinstitute.org/resources/reflections -july-2017.

to mean "anxiety," as it implies a concern that weighs down your spirit to the point where you feel like you're drowning.

When Peter says in 1 Peter 5:7 to cast "all your anxieties on him, because he cares for you," he is telling us to toss our anxieties out of our hearts and onto Jesus because he's strong enough to hold us *and them*. When you think too much about your cares, the worries weigh you down. Toss them onto the shoulders of the One who carries the universe.

Getting rid of anxiety, I've found, also delivers me from a bunch of other sins that anxiety produces. John Piper explains:

> Stop for a moment and think how many different sinful actions and attitudes come from anxiety. Anxiety about finances can give rise to coveting and greed and hoarding and stealing. Anxiety about succeeding at some task can make you irritable and abrupt and surly. Anxiety about relationships can make you withdrawn and indifferent and uncaring about other people. Anxiety about how someone will respond to you can make you cover over the truth and lie about things. So if anxiety could be conquered, a lot of sins would be overcome.[45]

Anxiety comes from thinking too much about the problem and too little about God. The good life is walking with God in freedom and joy, knowing that he is aware of

---

45. John Piper, "Battling the Unbelief of Anxiety," *Desiring God* (blog), September 25, 1988, https://www.desiringgod.org/messages/battling-the-unbelief-of-anxiety.

your burden and is carrying it for you better than you can carry it for yourself.

2. Anxiety Minimizes How Much God Thinks of Us (Matthew 6:26,30)

God doesn't care. I'm all alone. I'll never make it.

Anxious people struggle with those kinds of thoughts whenever they see no immediate solution to their problems. That anxiety then morphs into hopelessness, leading to coping strategies and self-medication, which sometimes lead to addiction and even (in extreme cases) to despair for living.

But here's the thing: *those statements are not true.* God could never forget or neglect one of his children.

After Jesus tells us to consider how well God takes care of the birds, he says, "Are you not of more value than they?" And after talking about how beautiful God made the flowers, Jesus says, "But if God so clothes the grass of the field, which today is alive and tomorrow is thrown into the oven, will he not much more clothe you, O you of little faith?" (Matthew 6:30). This is an argument from the lesser (birds and begonias) to the greater (you and me).

In other words, if God is the kind of God who cares about the safety of birds and the beauty of flowers in creation, don't you think he cares about you? Humans are of infinitely more value than birds and flowers. We are made in the image of God, and God cared enough about us to become human and die for us.

In Luke 12:32, Jesus goes the other way, arguing from the greater to the lesser. If God loved you enough to send Jesus to die for your sins (the greater), don't you think God knows your day-to-day needs (the lesser)?

The apostle Paul put it this way: "He who did not spare his own Son but gave him up for us all, how will he not also with him graciously give us all things?" (Romans 8:32).

Ask yourself: what more would God have to do to prove his loving commitment to you? This reminds me of how my kids, when they were younger, used to pester Veronica and me on family vacations. After spending the day at Disney World, we'd be thirty minutes behind our normal dinner schedule. Then my kids would say, "Dad, are we not going to eat?"

And I'd say, "You think I brought you this whole way, stood on the asphalt for nine hours in the scorching heat surrounded by tens of thousands of people to show you a good time, just to starve you for the next meal? Isn't just being here, walking around what feels like the surface of the sun packed uncomfortably with throngs of people, proof of my commitment to you? Do you know how much it cost to get you here? Do you think I'm standing in a two-hour line to ride Dumbo for ninety seconds *for my sake*? Surely if I cared enough to bring you on vacation, I care enough to keep you fed."

Sigh. Having kids on vacation is awesome. (Side note: I stopped calling those trips "vacations" because I came back mad that no "vacating" had happened. Instead I came home emotionally exhausted. So to manage my own expectations, I changed the nomenclature to "family trips." Now when I come back from vacation—er, a family trip—more tired than when I left, I am not so frustrated.)

I imagine God feels the same kind of exasperation with us sometimes. God sent his Son to a cross to die in humiliation for our sins—but we can't trust him with our bills, our families, our futures?

Worrying, for the Christian, is inherently *irrational*. It implies that God can take you to heaven, but he can't handle your life here on earth; that God is good for eternity but insufficient for today; that he delivered us from eternal torment but can't help us escape the difficulty of our circumstances.[46]

You've got to choose—you either believe in the God of the Bible who says he sovereignly manages all things for your good and promises to provide all your needs . . . or you don't.

Jesus says in Matthew 6:32 that it's the Gentiles (that is, the pagans and unbelievers) who worry about all these things. In other words, "Worrying is acting like an atheist!" Atheists worry about these things—and for good reason. Their belief structure means it's all, ultimately, on them.

---

46. Adapted from Tony Evans, "Reversing Anxiety Consequences: Matthew 6:25–34," February 28, 2021, YouTube video, https://www.youtube.com/watch?v=S95lfdu-sn8.

The Christian should think differently. We have a sovereign God unwaveringly committed to our good.

So say whatever you want, but your worry expresses what you really believe.

Which brings me back to how I started this chapter—the fact that I am *commanded* not to worry. Four times in our text in Matthew, Jesus commands us not to worry. And get this: "Fear not" is the most repeated command in the Bible, appearing 366 times. In other words, there's a "fear not" command for you every day of the year, including leap year.

I love it. God doesn't say, "Stop worrying, you dummy. It's a rule. Just follow it." No, he shows us *why* and *how* to overcome worry. He paints a picture of his faithfulness, then says, "Lean on me. Trust in me. Let my love drive out that fear. Cast all those worries upon me, and I'll handle them."

And we can. Because he can.

Paul says in Philippians 4:6, "In everything by prayer and supplication with thanksgiving let your requests be made known to God."

Let's break that down to simple, straightforward, bite-sized imperatives.

- Take everything to God—not just some things or the hard things, but all things.
- Pray with the awareness that you are talking with a God who loves you more than you love yourself.

- Be humble before God, not demanding. Trust him to know what's best.
- Be thankful and gracious, showing that you believe he will answer your request. It's impossible to say thanks if you don't trust him to answer.
- Make your requests known to God, then *know* that God knows and won't ever stop knowing. Period.

The kind of prayer Paul is talking about here means laying down your problems at Jesus's feet and leaving them there. It does you no good to tell God about your problems if you don't leave them with him. Often our prayer times are sessions where we worry out loud before God. God doesn't want us to merely inform him of our problems, but trust him with them.

3. Anxiety Is a False Prophet (Matthew 6:27,34)

In verse 27, Jesus reasoned with the crowd of worrywarts: The majority of what you worry about never comes to pass, so anxiety is interest paid on a debt that usually doesn't exist.

Furthermore, anxiety does nothing to change whatever it is we are worried about. Anxiety exists only in our hearts and does not do anything to affect the situation we're worried about. Look at Jesus's question in this verse: "And which of you by being anxious can add a single hour to his span of life?" Will worry add anything to your life? No. Ironically, if anything, it will just shorten it. Doctors point out that 75 to 90 percent of all doctor visits are stress- or anxiety-related.[47]

Dr. Charles Mayo of the famed Mayo Clinic said, "Worry affects circulation, the heart and the glands, the whole nervous system, and profoundly affects the heart. I have never known a man who died from overwork, but many who died from [worry]."[48]

I saw a bumper sticker one time that said, "Anxiety is my daily cardio." Anxiety certainly yields cardiac impact, but it's not usually the good kind.

So why does anxiety feel like the right response to our troubles and trials?

I can speak for myself. Worrying about stuff always makes me feel like I'm doing something. By devoting energy to anxiety, I feel actively engaged with whatever I am worried about. But as we all know, stewing about a problem isn't the same as fixing it.

Worrying won't affect anything except your health (negatively). Trusting Jesus with your worries, however, brings peace to you and solutions to your problems.

I once heard a leadership coach explain how in the early days of his start-up company, he hired one of those "virtual

47. "The Effects of Stress on Your Body," webmd.com, December 8, 2021, https://www.webmd.com/balance/stress-management/effects-of-stress-on-your-body.

48. Harvey Mackay, "Worry is a destructive habit in life, business," StarTribune.com, March 29, 2020, https://www.startribune.com/mackay-worry-is-a-destructive-habit-in-life-business/569165792/.

assistants" from India. Each night at five o'clock, he'd email her a list of assignments to complete throughout the night (since their days and nights were opposite). As the founder of this start-up, he was worried about so many things with the company—but each morning at eight o'clock, he said, he loved to get the little email from her: "Mr. So-and-So, here are all the things you asked me to do, completed and ready for your attention."

One afternoon, on a whim, he added this to her daily to-do list: "Please worry for me about meeting payroll, customers sharing our product with their friends, and retail stores featuring our product."

The next morning, he said, he was delighted to receive an email from his assistant in India that said, "Sir, I just want you to know I stayed up all night, while you slept, worried sick about those problems, and now I am putting them back in your very capable hands."

The founder said, "I began to do this regularly, and I don't know what it was, but just knowing she was worried about things when I went home helped me sleep better. In the morning I took whatever problem back over, but letting her worry in my place helped me rest better."

That's an interesting mental trick, but the Christian has someone to *really* hand burdens to when the workday is over. The Christian can sleep peacefully through the night, knowing the very capable hands of the heavenly Father have everything under control.

Furthermore, anxiety is a false prophet because the bulk of what we worry about never takes place. Think about how many things you worry about that never happen. (Hint: It's most of them.)

Look at how Jesus addresses this in verse 34: "Therefore do not be anxious about tomorrow, for tomorrow will be anxious for itself." I think, *Well, that's exactly what I was worried about—tomorrow!* But guess what will also be there tomorrow? God. And the God who gives you strength today will give you strength tomorrow. He won't deal with the 999 things that don't happen, but he will give you the strength to deal with the one or two that do.

God taught this to the children of Israel through his provision of manna for them in the wilderness. A desert is not known for its food supply. Yet almost every day, God provided little vitamin-packed, Ritz Cracker–looking things called "manna" for them to eat. The word *manna* literally means "whatever it is." The Israelites weren't sure what it was, but it satisfied their food needs day after day. Every morning (except for the Sabbath) they woke up, grabbed a bunch of manna, and ate it all day. They made manna-cotti, ba-manna bread.[49] All the best stuff. However, the rule was they could only gather enough for *that day*. If they tried to stockpile it, it would go bad and breed worms. (The

---

49. With credit to singer/songwriter Keith Green from "So You Wanna Go Back to Egypt?" 1980 Birdwing Music.

exception was on the morning before the Sabbath day, when they were told to gather two days' worth. Miraculously, it wouldn't go bad that night.[50])

What was God teaching the Israelites? Don't worry about tomorrow. I'll provide what you need when you need it. Your "daily bread." I'll send more "whatever it is" for whatever you need tomorrow.

Our minds explore every possible what-if . . .

What if I get robbed? What if I lose my job? What if my 401(k) crashes? What if I'm falsely accused at work? What if my kids want nothing to do with me? What if my wife gets cancer? What if I never get married? What if . . .

Realistically, you can do nothing about these hypothetical scenarios because, for the most part, these things are out of your control anyway. If something is beyond your control, worrying about it won't give you any more power.

Especially if you know someone who does have it under control.

You see, not only is worry foolish; it's also completely unnecessary. You don't have to worry because you know that God, who is faithful, promises to be present with you just as much tomorrow as he is today. He's looking over at you, saying, "Hey, trust me! I've been with you before, remember? And I'll be just as present in your tomorrow as I was in your yesterday. Friend, I got this!"

---

50. Exodus 16:22-26.

So instead of worrying about what you don't know and what you can't control, replace those anxious thoughts with what you *do* know:

- God sees.
- God cares.
- God never stops working.
- Not one molecule is out of his control.

In his book *The Salt-Cellars*, Charles Spurgeon repeated this adage from Baptist preacher Alexander McLaren: "Anxiety does not empty to-morrow of its sorrows, but only empties to-day of its strength."[51]

Whatever tomorrow holds, God will be there to give you daily strength. Stop listening to false prophets. In the Old Testament they stoned false prophets; we should take equally dramatic action against our anxiety.

Turn your attention to the one true prophet—the prophet who never lies, never fails, and always keeps his promises—*Jesus*.

Jesus was not just a prophet who told the truth—he was the God-man who took everything we were afraid of and absorbed it into his own body on the cross. That same God now tells us to trust him with everything we face.

Fill your mind with Jesus, and you'll have no room in there for worry. "Seek first the kingdom of God and his

---

51. C. H. Spurgeon, *The Salt-Cellars: Being a Collection of Proverbs, Together With Homely Notes Thereon* (New York: A. C. Armstrong and Son, 1889), 62.

righteousness, and all these things will be added to you" (Matthew 6:33).

Instead of seeking false prophets that waste your time, seek him. Instead of worrying about your life, focus on communing with him through worship and prayer, saturating yourself in Scripture and surrounding yourself with people who are walking this journey of faith with you.

The answer to worry is not a trouble-free life but trust in an almighty and always-caring God.

9

How Could a Loving God Send People to Hell?

Let me just jump right into it: for many, the idea of hell is proof that what Christians believe about God is not true. In fact, they see hell as some sort of "aha" contradiction within Christianity that overturns the whole system. *You talk about a loving, forgiving, graceful God, but then you say your God sends people to hell? Impossible!*

For many, hell makes God seem like a cruel, sadistic being who delights in our torture. It feels unjust. We all make a few mistakes in life, sure. Nobody's perfect . . . but then *hell?* The punishment exceeds the crime.

Some will begrudgingly consent to hell for a few of the worst. Hitler deserves hell. Jeffrey Dahmer, maybe. Terrorists and child abusers. But it's usually a smallish list.

Maybe hell is a relic of the Old Testament God, some people think—when God was mean and cranky—God in his middle school years, before he went through his PR makeover and re-presented himself as Jesus, meek and mild. Or, more likely, hell was something powerful Christians made up to keep people in line. It surprises many to learn that Jesus spoke more about hell than anyone else in the Bible. In fact, he spoke more about hell than about heaven!

Bottom line: hell is an important and prominent part of biblical teaching, and few things are less popular in the Christian message today. For many, hell is the *primary* obstacle keeping them from belief.

Honestly, I get it. In college, I went through a crisis of faith that arose from this issue. It paralyzed me. I felt like I had more compassion for other people than God did. After all, I wouldn't wish an eternal hell on my enemies. Even C. S. Lewis admitted, "There is no doctrine which I would more willingly remove from Christianity than [hell], if it lay in my power."[52]

I'm right there with him. Give me an eraser and ten minutes, and I'd get the hell out of the Bible. When I stop and think about hell and what eternal suffering must be like, I wince. My stomach hurts.

Yet despite what I and others may desire, hell is real. You see, if Jesus really is Lord, then what he said about eternity is true. Jesus's teaching is not a salad bar where you take the items you like and leave the rest. Jesus is either true in all that he says, or he's not. Lord of all, or not Lord at all.

After years of wrestling with the fairness of this concept, I've come to a little more peace with it—though I still have

---

52. C. S. Lewis, *The Problem of Pain* (New York: HarperOne, 1996), 119–20.

lots of questions. But through humble, open-minded study of the Scriptures and pleading with God for wisdom, I have learned more of the Bible's internal logic for why it is necessary. One of the passages that has helped me is the profound story Jesus tells about hell in Luke 16.

A True Story about Hell

One of Jesus's primary teaching devices was the parable, which is basically a fictional story with an eternal truth. Usually, his parables were not based on real people because the person was not as important as the point the parable made. That's why, in most parables, Jesus didn't use names.

This story of Lazarus and the rich man, however, broke the parable rules. First, it used a real person's name, a beggar named Lazarus. (All other parables describe the people as "the sower" or "the servant" or "the king.") Plus, neither Jesus nor Luke calls this story a parable. That has led many to conclude that this is not a parable, but a true story.

Here's how it goes:

> There was a rich man who was clothed in purple and fine linen and who feasted sumptuously every day. And at his gate was laid a poor man named Lazarus, covered with sores, who desired to be fed with what fell from the rich man's table. Moreover, even the dogs came and licked his sores. The poor man died and was carried by the angels to Abraham's

side. The rich man also died and was buried, and in Hades, being in torment, he lifted up his eyes and saw Abraham far off and Lazarus at his side. And he called out, "Father Abraham, have mercy on me, and send Lazarus to dip the end of his finger in water and cool my tongue, for I am in anguish in this flame." But Abraham said, "Child, remember that you in your lifetime received your good things, and Lazarus in like manner bad things; but now he is comforted here, and you are in anguish. And besides all this, between us and you a great chasm has been fixed, in order that those who would pass from here to you may not be able, and none may cross from there to us." And he said, "Then I beg you, father, to send him to my father's house—for I have five brothers— so that he may warn them, lest they also come into this place of torment." But Abraham said, "They have Moses and the Prophets; let them hear them." And he said, "No, Father Abraham, but if someone goes to them from the dead, they will repent." He said to him, "If they do not hear Moses and the Prophets, neither will they be convinced if someone should rise from the dead." (Luke 16:19–31)

What do we know about the man in hell? First, he's religious. We know that because he calls Abraham his father. He prays—that's right, he prays from hell—but notice that he prays not to God but to *Father Abraham*.

What is the significance of that? Jesus is making the point that this man was religious but had no actual relationship with God. Jesus tells this story in front of the Pharisees because he's making this point to them: *Your life is filled with religion, but you don't know God at all.*

Second, the man in the story was very rich while alive, but like many Pharisees, he was callous to the needs of suffering people around him. He wanted to have God *and* money, but when push came to shove, he was willing to compromise obedience to God to hold on to his precious money. Care for the poor is always a sign in the Bible of truly knowing God.

A Place Full of Fire

In Jesus's story, hell is depicted as a place full of fire (as it is in numerous other places in the Bible). A lot of people ask if the flames in hell are real. I read them as so, but *even if* the Bible uses flames here as a metaphor, keep in mind that the spiritual reality it points to would not be *less* intense, but *worse* than the physical representation of it.

Fire indicates insatiable desire. A fire consumes and consumes and consumes, devouring everything in its path, unsatisfied until nothing is left. In hell, you never get what you crave, what your heart burns to obtain. People go to hell because they are convinced they need something in life more than God. In this story, the rich man sought that satisfaction in the things of the earth—pleasures, addictions, money—and in the end, it all turned to nothing. Hell was simply the final, eternal stop on the empty and worthless trajectory this man had chosen for himself. His heart forever burned with the lust for material things he had dedicated his life to pursuing.

Which addresses one of people's primary objections to hell—that hell is a place full of people heartbroken over their sin, crying out in repentance to a God who won't listen anymore. Notice, the man in the parable never pleads to get out of hell; all he asks for is satisfaction and relief from pain. A drop of cool water. He never cries out in repentance or asks God to be restored to him. Revelation 22 makes clear that the people in hell never repent from their sin. God says, "He that is unjust, let him be unjust still" (verse 11 KJV). In other words, the fire of their burning desire for things to replace God in their heart never goes away. People in hell hate the experience of it, but they hate the concept of total submission to God even more.

In *The Great Divorce*, C. S. Lewis depicts a bus full of people from hell coming to visit heaven, which is awash in God's glory. At the end of the day, they *want* to go back to hell. As bad as hell is, with all its torments, they'd still rather be there than in a place filled with God's glory. You see, the essence of heaven is not streets of gold, just as the essence of hell is not fire. The essence of heaven is God; the essence of hell is his absence.

Hell is also described as a place of darkness. Darkness indicates the total absence of God. God is light, and God shines his light into our lives through good things both big and small—like the beauties of nature, friendship, art, and the aroma of a fresh cup of coffee in the morning. If God's not in hell, then nothing there reflects his glory, which results in complete and total darkness.

Hell is the fulfillment of a lifelong desire to keep God out of your life. You tell God "no" enough times that he finally consents. Or, to quote C. S. Lewis, if you won't say to God "Thy will be done," then he'll say to you, "Thy will be done."[53]

God takes no pleasure in this. In fact, Scripture says God didn't intend hell for us at all. He made it for the devil and the demons who had waged cosmic war against him (Matthew 25:41). Those who go to hell are those who participate in the Satanic rebellion of "I know better than God." Hell is a door, I've heard it said, first locked *from the inside*.

Let me go all theologian on you for a minute. In the Bible, we see both "passive" and "active" dimensions to the wrath of God. God's passive wrath is experienced simply as God leaving us to the painful consequences of our own choices. His active wrath is when he adds his own punishment to that choice. His active wrath is usually only an extension of, or an intensification of, his passive wrath. The rich man desired a life without God and chose that on earth. God gave him that in fullness in eternity.

---

53. Lewis, C.S. 1898-1963, *The Great Divorce: A Dream* (New York, HarperOne, 2001)

At the end of the day, God doesn't send anyone to hell. We send ourselves.

Many atheists, such as Friedrich Nietzsche, confess they would rather go into nothingness than surrender to God's will.[54] Others may never verbalize it that overtly, yet they freely acknowledge they don't want to completely and totally submit to anyone.

Marilynne Robinson hit the nail on the head in her novel *Gilead*: "If you want to inform yourselves as to the nature of hell, don't hold your hand in a candle flame, just ponder the meanest, most desolate place in your [own] soul."[55]

Getting the *Hell* Out of You

People ask, "But I thought God was love? Where is the love amid this hell business? Hitler, I get; he's in hell. Someone who raped and killed a child, definitely. But cheating on my taxes gets me eternity alongside Charles Manson? I'm a good person!"

Hold on a second. The Bible says the essence of sin is something we are all guilty of—rejecting the Godness of God. The really *wicked* part of sin is not the grotesque things that make the six o'clock news, but defying God's

54. Friedrich Nietzsche, *Beyond Good and Evil*, trans. Helen Zimmern (Serenity Publishers, 2010), https://www.marxists.org/reference /archive/nietzsche/1886/beyond-good-evil/ch03.htm.
55. Marilynne Robinson, *Gilead*, (New York: Picador, 2004), 208.

authority and usurping his role as the most important Being in the universe. How we express that rebellion—whether in polite, socially acceptable ways or monstrous, raging ways—is less important.

If our lives are lived in that posture of rebellion, then even the so-called "good" things we did in our life don't seem to be all that good. Let me give you an example. Let's say you found out your husband was having an affair. A private investigator tipped you off. You follow your husband to a hotel lobby where he is meeting his mistress, and as you peek out from behind the hotel plants, you notice he tips the bellhop. A genuinely good deed. But in the context of something horribly bad, it's hard to call this act "good."

Or let's say you have two terrorists building a bomb to blow up a bus full of schoolchildren. As they work, one realizes the other forgot his sandwich, so he shares his sandwich with him. Again, another genuinely kind deed. But in light of the horrific circumstance in which this "good" deed takes place, it's hard to call it "good."

The fact that we don't center our lives on God and worship him is cosmic adultery worthy of the severest punishment. Romans 5:10 actually calls us "enemies" of God, like those terrorists are to us. Even our genuinely good deeds on earth are done in the context of a life of unspeakable injustice and wickedness.

But you say, "Okay, I understand we're all guilty. But why the infliction of *eternal* torment? Isn't that too harsh a retribution for what I've done?"

It helps here to think less about *what* you've done and more about *who* you've done it against. Certain sins increase in seriousness relative to who they are committed against. For example, if you kick a dog, you could be fined. But kick a guy on the street and you might go to jail for a few weeks. Walk up and attempt a roundhouse kick on the King of England, and you're likely to be in jail for years and years and years. Hell is infinite because our sin is against an infinite God of infinite glory—the King of all kings—so justice demands an infinite punishment.

Hell is what hell is because God is who God is. Many theologians think they're doing God a favor by lessening hell, but really what they're doing is diminishing the greatness of God.

We think hell is severe because we don't think trampling on the glory of God is that big of a deal. We think the biggest deal in the universe is *us*. I know this is horribly offensive to us humans who think the universe is all about us, but we are not the center of the universe. The whole of creation is a theater for the only true, good, all-powerful One, God. He is the big deal in the universe, and everything works toward his glory. Hell itself is a permanent monument to the greatness of his name.

If you lessen hell, you lessen God's holiness and righteousness. Hell is what hell is because God is who God is.

You ask, "Where is the love in that for us?" The love is in God allowing us, if we choose, to enjoy and share in his glory by receiving his mercy. God loved us enough to endure hell and wrath itself on the cross, in our place: "God demonstrates his own love for us in this: While we were still sinners [enemies of God], *Christ died for us*" (Romans 5:8 NIV, italics mine).

Hell should make our mouths stand agape at the righteousness and holiness of God. It should make us tremble before his majesty and grandeur. And it should make us weep with gratitude that God, in his grace, provided a way of escape.

In the end, God doesn't just want to get us out of hell. God wants to take the hell out of us—and he does that by offering love to us. We have to choose one or the other—self-will and sin or surrender and Jesus.

What about Those Who Have Never Heard?

Finally, you ask, "What about those who have never heard the gospel? Do they go to hell? That hardly seems fair."

This is one of the toughest questions to grapple with. Scripture makes clear that no one is ever held responsible for what they haven't heard. We are only held responsible for what we have heard and rejected.

But all people have heard about God. Paul said that what can be known about God has been made plain to all people (Romans 1:19–20). Every human being, everywhere, has been made aware of God in two ways.

First, the glory and beauty of creation teaches us that there is a Creator. There is a natural, innate sense of awe and wonder as we look at creation. We look around and instinctively know we didn't come from nowhere. Creation screams at us the presence of a glorious, all-powerful Creator. We may convince our heads that other explanations exist for how we got here, but Paul says our hearts know the truth.

Second, the presence of an individual's conscience teaches each of us there is a Lawgiver. We innately know basic right and wrong. When your conscience tells you, "That's wrong," that's an indication of someone who established a law in you and to whom you ultimately must answer.

That there is a God is something we can't *not* know, Paul says. We all know he's there, and we've all rebelled against him, rejecting his authority and glory. For this, we all stand condemned (Romans 3:10–23). The gospel is an undeserved second chance (Romans 3:24).

But what about those people who look at the stars or into their hearts and want to know this God they see evidence of? Scripture indicates that if someone actually does that, God will send a messenger to them with the gospel. Consider the story of Cornelius in Acts 10–11. As God was preparing Cornelius to seek God, he was preparing Peter to share the gospel.

I have heard story after story of individuals, far removed from the Christian church, who began such a spiritual quest. (In fact, I've been a part of a few of those stories.) God leads them to a Bible, a church, a believer. Trust me: God wants people to believe more than we do, and he frequently moves mountains to reach them. In eternity, no one will be able to point their finger at God and say he was unfair. No one will say, "I wanted to know you, but you wouldn't have me." All of us, in eternity, will sing the song of Moses, which says, "Just and true are your ways, O King of the nations!" (Revelation 15:3).

At the end of the day, God doesn't force a relationship on any of us. He gives us a choice. When it's all said and done, if you step off this earth into hell, fists still clenched against God, Jesus's voice will still be calling out to you: "You don't have to do this."

What's Really Unfair

I was once sharing Christ with an intelligent young lady who had never had someone explain the gospel to her. I explained to her how Jesus died for our sin and offered salvation to all who would receive it.

She said to me, "Wait a minute. You're telling me that if people do not receive Jesus, they will not spend eternity in heaven but in hell?" I said, "Yes, that is what I am saying." She said, "I don't think you actually believe that." I told her, "Of course I do." She said, "Well, you don't *act* like you believe it." I replied, "What do you mean? I'm sitting here telling you about it and trying to convince you it's true."

"No," she said. "You're acting like you're trying to win a debate with me. If I really believed what you say you do, I do not know how I would make it through the day. I would continually have tears in my eyes, and I'd be pleading with every person I meet to come to Jesus. I'm not sure how I would emotionally survive, but I do know that all of my life priorities would be different."

I knew she was right. I knew that my lazy, noncommittal way of sharing the gospel was inconsistent with what I believed about the reality of heaven and hell.

Here's an honest question for you to consider: have you fully wrestled with the implications of the gospel—that God has provided a way of escape from hell in Jesus, but only if one chooses to receive it?

> "How then will they call on him in whom they have not believed? And how are they to believe in him of whom they have never heard? And how are they to hear without someone preaching?" (Romans 10:14)

Pause for a moment to slowly read this description of hell by the eighteenth-century American preacher Jonathan Edwards. It's consistent with what Jesus described in Luke 16:

> . . . Imagine yourself to be cast into a fiery oven, or a great furnace. . . . Imagine also that your body were to lie there for a quarter of an hour, full of fire, and all the while full of quick sense; what horror would you feel at the entrance of such a furnace! and how long would that quarter of an hour seem to you! And after you had endured it for one minute, how overbearing would it be to you to think that you had it to endure the other fourteen!

But what would be the effect on your soul, if you knew you must lie there enduring that torment to the full for twenty-four hours! And how much greater would be the effect, if you knew you must endure it for a whole year; and how vastly greater still, if you knew you must endure it for a thousand years!—O then, how would your hearts sink, if you knew, that you must bear it for ever and ever! that there would be no end! that after millions of millions of ages, your torment would be no nearer to an end, and that you never, never should be delivered!

But your torment in hell will be immensely greater than this illustration represents. How then will the heart of a poor creature sink under it! How utterly inexpressible and inconceivable must the sinking of the soul be in such a case!

Who in your life needs to hear?

I understand the desire to believe that all roads lead to God and everyone gets saved in the end. However, that's not what Jesus taught. Hell is the final expression of God's justice against sin and the holiness of his character. Do you believe he is Lord? Then we must follow his teaching about hell. And live differently because of it.

Take a moment to sit silently and consider:

Every second, about two people die.

Every minute, 107 people die.

Every hour, 6,390 people die.

Every day, more than 153,000 people die.

Every year, 59 million people die.[56]

Jesus commissioned you to warn others about how they could escape from hell. First Timothy 2:4 tells us that God "desires all people to be saved and to come to the knowledge of the truth."

Is there anything in your life more important than that?

---

56. World death clock: https://www.medindia.net/patients/calculators /world-death-clock.asp https://worldpopulationreview.com/countries /deaths-per-day

10

How Should Christians Handle Political Differences?

And you thought the *last* chapter was challenging. Time to put on your theological big-kid pants now!

I need to keep things light here, so I'll open with some safe political jokes. Feel free to add your own *ba-dum-bump* at the end of each.

- The opposite of "pro" is "con," so the opposite of progress is . . . congress.

- It's been so cold in Chicago recently that city council members have actually been seen walking around Chicago with their hands in their *own* pockets.

- A robber held up a well-dressed man, pointing his gun and yelling, "Give me all your money!" The man replied, "Don't you know who I am? I'm a US congressman!" The robber retorted, "In that case, give me all *my* money!"

- Have you heard about the new presidential value meal at McDonald's? You order whatever you want, and the person after you has to pay for it.

For most people, politics is no longer a laughing matter. It doesn't matter what your political views are; I'm betting you approach political conversations with a pit in your stomach. You're wondering if this is the last chapter you'll read in this book. If I turn out to share your politics, then this is a great book you'll recommend to a friend! If I'm not, you wonder how you can take seriously anything else I say. Maybe you'll even create a fake persona on Twitter so you can hit me with some mean tweets.

Some context: I was born in 1973, during the waning years of Nixon and the transition to Ford. As a kid, I grew up during the tenures of Carter and Reagan and reached adulthood during George H. W. Bush's time in office. I became a pastor almost twenty-five years ago, around the time President Clinton was in office.

Politics was never a fun topic of conversation. But with each passing year, I've seen politics become more and more divisive, particularly in the church. For most people, their political affiliation has turned into an identity. Once you adopt a label, you assume a whole set of character traits. You listen only to certain news outlets. To the "other" side, you're either a Marxist or a socialist, or a radical, or a fascist, or an extremist.

Social media thrives on headlines. Those headlines need to encourage user clicks, so they use hyperbole (exaggeration) to get you to click on their account. Social media algorithms are set to reinforce what you believe, highlighting the extreme stupidity of your opponents. Most people voluntarily dial in for an hour or two every evening to have their favorite talk show host tell them how dumb and unreasonable people on the other side are.

This mania used to reach a crescendo only during presidential election seasons, meaning we braced ourselves every four years. Now it's every day, all day. Thank you, CNN and Fox News. I disciple people for one hour a weekend with the Bible, and Fox News and CNN get three hours every night. Is it any wonder that the church is divided?

As a pastor, my calling is to teach the Bible and make disciple-making disciples. That means I forgo answering a lot of important questions because I don't want my answers to keep people from hearing me on the things that really do matter: who Jesus is, what his mission is, and what that means for us. It's like a friend of mine says: "I *might* be wrong about the best response to global warming. But I'm *not* wrong about the gospel, and I don't want to let my opinions on the former keep people from hearing me on the latter."

That doesn't mean, of course, I will be silent about things the Bible speaks clearly about—the sanctity of human life, the equality of all people under the law, the importance of protecting our children, the importance of religious freedom, and God's designs for sex and gender, to name a few. I usually refrain from weighing in on things about which the Bible is *not* clear—topics about which sincere, Bible-believing Christians might genuinely disagree—and through which runs a dotted line (at best) between a biblical principle and its political application.

Questions like the best approaches to taxation, education, global warming, poverty relief, or foreign policy. Or questions about which candidate will do the best job for the country in a given season. Almost every election, you see, involves trade-offs; you like some things about one candidate's platform but not others, but you have to decide which issues are of greater importance in this election. You might agree with other believers on every single issue, but because you put them in a different order of importance, you land on different candidates. You may strongly disagree with another believer's "political calculus," but those issues usually aren't first orders of faith.

The world wants to know what flag we wave. "Are you Team Donkey or Team Elephant?" In ancient Israel, the Israelites called God *Jehovah Nissi*, which translates literally as "the Lord is my flag." That's the flag I'm waving. He's the banner I march behind.

Ultimately, we are not the party of the donkey or the elephant; we are the tribe of the Lamb. That doesn't mean we don't develop political opinions on the secondary questions, just that we don't associate them with the name of the church or the authority of God. Before I declare "This is how God feels" about something, I want a chapter and verse.

In John 18, leading up to Jesus's trial and crucifixion, we read that when the soldiers came to take Jesus prisoner in the garden of Gethsemane, Peter pulled out his sword and tried to take off the head of one of the mob. He missed, slicing off one of the servant's ears. But then Jesus (in one of my favorite scenes from his life) patiently reached down, picked up the guy's ear, and reattached it (Luke 22:50-51). What did Malchus, the guy who got an earful, think? He was there to arrest Jesus, but Jesus healed him. You can't be the same after that!

Jesus also had some words for Peter: "Put your sword back into its place. For all who take the sword will perish by the sword. Do you think that I cannot appeal to my Father, and he will at once send me more than twelve legions of angels?" (Matthew 26:52–53). Jesus was saying, "This kingdom I am bringing, Peter, does not depend on you using force, nor is it sustained by your sword."

Then we read that Jesus stood before Pilate, the Roman governor in charge, later that night. Pilate asked him: "Are you the king of the Jews?" To which Jesus responded: "My kingdom is not of this world. If my kingdom were of this world, my servants would have been fighting, that I might not be delivered over to the Jews. But my kingdom is not from the world" (John 18:33,36).

The Savior we hope in, the Savior we adore, the Savior to whom we pledge our first allegiance, did not bring a kingdom that would operate by the same rules as earthly kingdoms. Political and military weaponry are of little value sustaining or advancing Jesus's kingdom.

As Christians, we are citizens of a different nation. We march under a different flag.

So here's the question: how should Christians handle their secondary political differences? (Again, we're not talking about compromising on things the Bible speaks clearly about—only secondary questions about political applications over which a sincere Christian might genuinely find disagreement with another one.)

At Summit Church, I taught a sermon series titled "Four Myths Americans Believe about Politics" that provides a compass for navigating these questions. Let me share those points with you here.

Myth 1: Politics Are of *First* Importance

Let me be clear: Politics are indeed important—enacting good politics can be a way of loving your neighbor, promoting justice, and protecting the vulnerable. But most political *issues* are not of first importance. That's because the solutions humanity most needs start not in the Oval Office but the human heart. Thus, Jesus didn't come to preach policy change. He came to offer heart resurrection.

His approach was unique among religious leaders. Moses overthrew a country (Egypt), destroyed it from the inside, then marched off with a new set of rules for a new nation. Muhammad rode a white horse and conquered cities. Even Confucius and Buddha associated political aspirations with their religious reforms.

Jesus avoided all of that, even though he was constantly pushed toward it by both sides. He came, primarily, to reconcile people to God and transform them from within, not to install governments. The apostles did not run for office. Paul didn't go to Rome to reform the Roman Senate (which it desperately needed.) Jesus's followers found the lost and the forgotten and made them citizens of heaven.

The early church and the apostles operated not as a political organization but as a living, breathing organism— the body of Christ.

Jesus invited people from different political viewpoints into his closest group. Simon the Zealot would be called a nationalist today, maybe even a terrorist. Matthew, the tax collector, would be seen as a member of the rich, privileged class. Fishermen were the proletariat, the working class.

At the time, people were divided over Rome's occupation of Israel. Talks around the campfire could have included calling each other out and questioning their stance on Rome: "Are you Pro-Ro or No-Ro?" Maybe Simon was like, "Aw, not that pinko Commie Matthew," and Matthew was like, "Not that MAGA hat–wearing, knuckle-dragging Neanderthal Simon." And if you passed by their tent late at night, they'd probably have had their fingers in each other's faces as they argued.

But here's the point: the unity they found in Jesus super-seded their differences, and they ended up loving each other enough to die for each other, because the cause they rallied behind was more important than their political agendas.

This is why, as a pastor, I don't pontificate about many of my secondary political views. I know that if I discuss these things from the pulpit, what I say will be interpreted as representing the authority of the church, even if I give disclaimers about these being my own views. And that might keep people from hearing me on the one, essential commission God gave to me: to preach the gospel to all people.

You are likely different. If you're not a pastor, you have more freedom in expounding your political views because most people won't associate your view with that of the church. The Dutch theologian Abraham Kuyper distinguished between the church as an organism and the church as an organization.

As an organism, members of the church should permeate all walks of society, seeking to bring their Christian worldview to even the smallest questions of life.[57] As an organization, however, the church's calling is not politics, so its leaders should not generally associate the church's identity with a political ideology. Following the lead of Jesus (more on this below), we should show restraint in getting involved in political matters.

That means that if you don't represent the "church as organization" like I do, you have more freedom to be vocal about your viewpoints. Even so, don't buy into the myth that politics is of first importance. Know when to turn the political dial down so you can turn the gospel dial up.

I receive more angry emails about politics, from both sides, than all other issues put together. I wish I got more emails

---

57. https://blog.lexhampress.com/2015/11/16/20151116abraham
-kuyper-on-a-church-that-is-both-organism-and-institution/

about doubling our missionary force, planting more churches, raising up volunteers, caring for single moms, protecting the unborn, and recruiting more mentors for our prison ministry. Sadly, most of the angry emails argue that I'm not saying enough about the upcoming presidential race or suggest I should talk a little bit more about some issue. Our churches are dividing over politics, and for that we should grieve.

When you walk by your neighbors' house, and they have a sign in their yard promoting the other candidate, is your first instinct to think, *How could they be so dumb?* Or is your first thought, *I wonder if they know Jesus,* and then to pray for them?

Almost 60 percent of Americans say they don't have any close friends who vote differently from them.[58] That statistic by itself proves how much people believe this first myth.

Myth 2: Politics Are of *No* Importance

The second myth is the exact opposite of the first. Some believe politics have no importance in their lives. They say high-minded things like, "Jesus is my President" and avoid

---

58. C. K., "Is political polarisation cutting Thanksgiving dinners short?" *The Economist*, November 21, 2018, https://www.economist.com/democracy-in-america/2018/11/21/is-political-polarisation-cutting-thanksgiving-dinners-short?utm_medium=cpc.adword.pd&utm_source=google&ppccampaignID=17210591673&ppcadID=&utm_campaign=a.22brand_pmax&utm_content=conversion.direct-response.anonymous&gclid=Cj0KCQjw0vWnBhC6ARIsAJpJM6e6q5tGf0QtDYgk4L2ITlgFs5kPiyMmbMJL2Gg93vahBea1Ui2daKAaAvtREALw_wcB&gclsrc=aw.ds.

political processes altogether. This attitude also is a myth. And very unbiblical.

Joseph, Daniel, and Nehemiah worked within the political realm of their nations to see God accomplish great things and prosper his people during difficult times. Esther helped to thwart a mass destruction of Jews in Persia using her relationship with the king. From King David through his line of descendants, as the leader went, so also the nation followed. Good and faithful kings in Israel brought peace and prosperity, while evil and idolatrous kings brought destruction and chaos.

Practicing good politics is a way of loving your neighbor. God calls his people to be salt and light in every part of the world—from their own house to the White House. Politics matters because politics are a tangible way of loving our neighbors and shaping our world. We might not always know what policies work best, but we're called to use our wisdom and creativity in politics, just like we would in business, church, or our family.

Early activist Christians enshrined in the US Constitution things like individual freedom, religious liberty, the separation of powers, and government accountability. I'm glad Christians during that era didn't buy into this second myth. In fact, Christian historian David Barton found that the vast majority of the founding fathers' writing cited the Bible or were based on biblical principles.[59]

---

59. "Statements From Founding Fathers and Early Statesmen on Jesus, Christianity, and the Bible," Wall Builders, https://wallbuilders.com/founding-fathers-jesus-christianity-bible/.

State constitutions all mention God by name at least once, and between all fifty of them it totals with two hundred mentions overall.[60] If we attempt to draw a circle around politics and say, "Not relevant for Christians," we dishonor God and hurt our neighbors. Our freedoms, and most of our justice reforms (like women's suffrage and the Civil Rights Movement), were anchored in a biblical worldview. Christians need to be involved!

First Timothy 2:1–2 says, "First of all, then, I urge that supplications, prayers, intercessions, and thanksgivings be made for all people, for kings and all who are in high positions, that we may lead a peaceful and quiet life, godly and dignified in every way." Praying for our political leaders and seeking the peace and prosperity of our cities means working for justice and equality under the law, as well as promoting education, business, security, defense, and many other things.

Yes, politics should be important to a follower of God. Christians should desire to bring the Christian worldview into everything they think about, especially politics.

Just remember to balance this with the first myth and be humble when you're dealing with an application of a principle not directly spelled out in Scripture. Know when to give other Christians freedom to disagree. Christians should save their authoritative thunder for when they have

---

60. Aleksandra Sandstrom, "God or the divine is referenced in every state constitution," Pew Research Center, August 17, 2017, https://www.pewresearch.org/short-reads/2017/08/17/god-or-the -divine-is-referenced-in-every-state-constitution/.

a chapter and verse reference that gives them the confidence to say: "Thus says the Lord!"

Myth 3: I See Everything Clearly

In January 2019, Nicholas Sandmann—a student from Covington High School in Kentucky—was at the Lincoln Memorial on a class field trip. A tribe of Native Americans approached the group and began chanting while banging drums. You probably remember this because shortly afterward, a video of the incident appeared on Twitter and created a huge stir.

Why? Because Nicholas was wearing a MAGA hat and looking rather smug as the leader of the tribe chanted in his face. This sixteen-year-old became a target of attacks. Many Christian leaders, including me, publicly denounced his attitude on the airwaves.

There was just one problem. The incident wasn't quite so black-and-white. The media showed only a clip, then told us what to think. A longer clip showed that Nicholas wasn't the aggressor but a bystander who was trying to be respectful to a group that had ganged up on him. Nicholas reached settlements in lawsuits against NBC, CNN, and the *Washington Post* for their inaccurate reporting.

I was wrong to speak out definitively before I knew all the facts. I fell for the narrative others wrote. I didn't see the incident clearly, looking only through a lens tainted by contemporary biases.

That was a relatively small incident, but it proves a much broader point: church leaders in the past have fallen on the wrong side of political issues. Several famous British pastors were wrong on the justice and necessity of British imperialism in the world. Billy Graham went on record late in the Vietnam War endorsing both it and the trustworthiness of President Nixon. Several American church leaders, including Southern Baptist President W. A. Criswell, not only failed to support the cause of civil rights but also opposed it, calling it overly Marxist. Dr. Criswell later went on record saying, "Never had I been so blind."[61]

Jesus modeled for us what the right kind of restraint looks like. It's one of the most helpful incidents from his life on this subject. In Luke 12, he was asked to adjudicate a particular social justice complaint—in this case, a younger brother was accusing his older brother of leveraging his position to cheat him out of his rightful inheritance.

Note that this was a real problem in ancient Israel—a legitimate social justice complaint. Now, if you know *anything* about the life and ministry of Jesus, you know he cared about injustice. He preached against it all the time. He *condemned greedy exploitation*, particularly by the powerful against the weak. He went so far as to say in Luke 16:19–31 that those in positions of power who did not

---

61. Curtis W. Freeman, "'Never Had I Been So Blind': W. A. Criswell's 'Change' on Racial Segregation," *The Journal of Southern Religion* 10, (2007), 1–12, https://jsr.fsu.edu/Volume10/Freeman.pdf.

use that power to lift others up were in danger of hellfire, regardless of the fervency of their religion. So, suffice it to say, he cares about injustice.

Yet in the situation with the brothers, instead of giving a specific—you might even say political—answer to this question, Jesus withholds his opinion. He says, rather starkly, "Man, who made me a judge or arbitrator over you?" (Luke 12:14). In other words, "Is this what I was sent here to do?" And then, instead of playing judge and jury, he warns *both* brothers (and everyone listening) about the idolatry of money that threatens to condemn them both.

Why did Jesus respond this way? Well, had he rendered judgment on this case, he would have cut off half of his audience from his life-saving message (whichever half agreed with the brother he sided against). And after that, Jesus probably would have had a line a mile long of people wanting him to adjudicate their cases, which would have kept him from his essential calling: to seek and save the lost. He showed restraint in adjudicating the particulars of this case so he could preach the gospel to all.

The wave of violence tied to social justice got many pastors in trouble here in the US. On the one hand, who wouldn't want justice and fairness for all people? However, the narrative was tied into an anti-police rhetoric that was often downright hateful. I tried to think about this as a pastor, which meant I was always keenly aware that I have both people of color and first responders in my congregation (and many who are both). If I chose to take a hasty stand with one side, it would look like I didn't care about the other side. It was a difficult season, for sure. Eventually, I brought representatives of the two groups together (both people of color and police), and we had one of the most moving, healing conversations I've ever been a part of in my twenty-five years in ministry. Sometimes all we need for unity is a broadened perspective.

Satan loves a divided world that swirls with chaos because he can more easily master it. If we really want to put a thumb in the devil's eye, we'll remind ourselves that we don't always know all the facts. And we'll remember what my mom often told me: you have *two* ears and *one* mouth for a reason. James, Jesus's half brother, has been right all along: "Know this, my beloved brothers: let every person be quick to hear, slow to speak, slow to anger" (James 1:19).

Myth 4: My Party Is the Party of God

The terms *left* and *right* for political parties all started in 1789 because of seating arrangements. Members of the French National Assembly were divided as they drafted a constitution.[62] One faction, the anti-royalist revolutionaries, seated themselves on the left of the presiding officer, while the more conservative supporters of the monarchy sat on the

---

62. Madeleine Carlisle, "What to Know About the Origins of 'Left' and 'Right' in Politics, From the French Revolution to the 2020 Presidential Race," *Time*, September 14, 2019, https://time .com/5673239/left-right-politics-origins/1789.

right. Today, when you see speeches in congress, the parties are strategically seated, usually in groups on one side or the other.

I know, I know . . . on judgment day, the Bible says one group will be on Jesus's right and the other will be on Jesus's left, and the ones on the right go right to heaven and the ones on the left go to hell (Matthew 25:31-46). But that is not Jesus taking a side. His left and right have nothing to do with our political left and right. Nor is the fact that Jesus rode into Jerusalem on a donkey his implicit endorsement of the Democrats.

Jesus was clear that his kingdom is not of this world, which means no political party completely represents the Jesus party. Earthly institutions are always tainted by sin. Both left and right fall short of the glory of God.

Joshua, leader of the Israelites, encountered an angel of the Lord while prepping for war against another nation. He asked the angel, "Are you for us, or for our adversaries?" The angel replied, "No; but I am the commander of the army of the LORD" (Joshua 5:13–14).

Neither God nor Jesus nor any angel is for either side of today's political parties. Both get certain things right; both have their own sinful proclivities. You may feel one party is closer to truth and justice than another. That's fine—vote according to your conscience. God's people are not synonymous with any political party; they are identified only by him. He's our banner, and that means we are on the side of all things justice, regardless of whether that particular justice issue is usually associated with our faction.

God isn't even pro-America—as in, America is his chosen people at the expense of other nations. I do believe America's freedoms are good things, divine things, perhaps even the best application of the New Testament's indirect instructions on political structures in human history.

I believe God wants to use the resources and people of the United States to reach the world for Christ. I love my country and I'll sing the national anthem vigorously with my hand over my heart, and I get teary-eyed reading some of the old war stories about great battles. I love the flag, my mom, and apple pie. But I don't love America *in spite of* other nations, nor do I believe the importance of America's "mission in the world" comes anywhere close to the importance of Jesus's mission to the lost.

Just as Jesus told Peter to put away his sword, he would say the same to us. The hope of the world is not found in the stars and stripes but in the scars and stripes on our Savior's back. God's kingdom is not in Washington, D.C., but at the throne of heaven where Jesus reigns.

Please vote, but remember that you are a citizen, ultimately, of a greater kingdom. Election Day does not compare to judgment day, when every knee will bow and every tongue will confess who is really in charge.

What would happen if today's Christians were as passionate about seeing people come to Jesus as they were about political victories? I'm not sure there's any idol that so threatens the soul of the church in America as much as the lure of political power, nor any poison that so corrupts our witness as the self-righteousness that comes from despising the other side.

I'm convinced that both Democrats and Republicans need Jesus. People shouting "Black Lives Matter" need Jesus. People responding with "Blue Lives Matter" need Jesus. Liberals and conservatives need Jesus. Public school teachers need Jesus. Homeschoolers need Jesus.

If Christians preached the gospel, declared Jesus as King, and lived out his mission, then we'd see the culture of this world change, from families to schools to the arts to businesses—and yes, even to politics.

That's what I vote for every day.

11

Why Does God Care So Much About My Sex Life?

I don't do diets very well. I've half-heartedly tried a few throughout my life—keto, paleo, Atkins, intermittent fasting, the flexitarian, and the eat-a-bunch-of-carbs-and-gain-lots-of-weight diet. My doctor recently gave me the "you really need to pay better attention to your saturated fat consumption" talk, so now I'm trying to cut out as much sugar as possible. I have a thirty-year-old friend who eats only a twelve-ounce ribeye *every* night for dinner and swears it is good for his health. I swear he feels that way because he's thirty.

God, in the Old Testament, was concerned about what his people ate. Leviticus 11 detailed the kosher diet. From this list, the Jews labeled foods "clean" and "unclean."

When you look at the diet in Leviticus 11, you think, *Okay, so vulture, weasel, bat, and rat are off my diet. I'm good with that. Oh, but wait, the pig! And shrimp! Eating bacon-wrapped shrimp is a sin? Surely Moses got a bit hasty there.*

Diets work until you have to consistently say no to something you want.

When your body craves something forbidden to you, that's when you focus on the *why* of the diet: to lose weight, to live longer, to see your grandkids get married, to get off meds, to live pain-free, to be able to see your shoes, etc. Then the diet has a clear purpose.

Which brings us to . . . sex, also something we love to consume because it feels good. A few chapters after the kosher diet, God outlines a number of sexual relations we must avoid. And for some of us, these guidelines feel just as irrelevant as the food prescriptions (Leviticus 18).

The apostle Paul made clear that the Old Testament's dietary prescriptions of eating food offered to idols were no longer binding (1 Corinthians 8:4-6), but that the broad strokes of its prescriptions on sex were. All sexual sin (which he defined as any kind of sex other than between two people of the opposite sex within the bounds of marriage) was bad not just for society but also for the soul (1 Corinthians 5:9-10; 6:12–20; 7:1-5).

God cares about your sex life because, as with food, "you are what you eat." Just as your physical health is directly related to your consumption of food, your spiritual health is directly related to your sexual consumption.

Our society loves to talk about sex as if it were just a biological urge to satisfy, not altogether different from eating a cookie when we're hungry. Others see it as a sport: "Let's go out and find a partner to play a couple matches, just like tennis, touch football, or baseball, which also involves getting to first, second, or third base. We'll just have fun. No big deal."

In the 1975 film *Love and Death*, the character Sonja (Diane Keaton), says, "Sex without love is an empty experience." To which Boris, played by Woody Allen, responds, "Yes, but as empty experiences go, it's one of the best."[63]

In other words, "What's the big deal since sex is just the satisfaction of a physical craving? We're only having a little fun."

But we all know that's not true. We *know* sex isn't just physical. Consider these insightful questions posed by Andy Stanley:[64]

- If sex is just physical, why is rape so much more harmful to a woman than simply being beaten up? Women will report physical abuse much more often than they will rape. There's something deeply and personally uncomfortable about it.

- Why is it that when a child is sexually abused and then becomes an adult and connect the dots, it is so difficult to shake off the abuse? It's not just that

---

63. *Love and Death*, director Woody Allen, 1975, DVD.
64. Andy Stanley, *The New Rules for Love, Sex, and Dating* (Grand Rapids: Zondervan, 2015.

an authority figure betrayed them. No, the wound goes much deeper.

- Why is it that men with the deepest sexual issues often had uninvolved or missing fathers?
- Why are most people's greatest regrets so often sexual? (When somebody comes to me and says, "Pastor, I have to tell you something I have never told anybody else. . . ." It's almost always sexual.)
- To these, I would add: Why is adultery so devastating to a marriage?

The question now isn't whether sex matters. We all know it does. The bigger question is: what is the difference between healthy and unhealthy sexuality?

More than Just Mammals

According to the apostle Paul, sex corresponds with the depths of who we are because God built our sexuality as a way of learning about his love for humanity. Consider these verses:

> Husbands should love their wives as their own bodies. He who loves his wife loves himself. For no one ever hated his own flesh, but nourishes and cherishes it, just as Christ does the church, because we are members of his body. "Therefore a man shall leave his father and mother and hold fast to his wife, and the two shall become one flesh." This mystery

is profound, and I am saying that it refers to Christ and the church. (Ephesians 5:28–32)

Or this from 1 Corinthians: "Flee from sexual immorality. Every other sin a person commits is outside the body, but the sexually immoral person sins against his own body" (1 Corinthians 6:18).

Paul wrote this to Corinth, a city in Greece: population twenty-five thousand, of which nearly one thousand were prostitutes.[65] The most famous temple in the city was dedicated to the goddess Aphrodite, and people worshiped her by having sex with one of those prostitutes. People in Corinth saw sex as a spiritual yearning to be cultivated and expressed.

Paul, in seeking to refute this mentality, quoted from a Corinthian proverb about sex: "Food is meant for the stomach and the stomach for food" (1 Corinthians 6:13), which suggested that just as food satisfied the cravings of the body, so sex satisfies the cravings of the loins. (Same argument you hear today! But no, Paul said. The body isn't built that way. The body is intimately connected to the soul. What you do with your body, you do with your soul—your very self.

God designed sex (physical oneness with someone) to be experienced in a context of oneness in every other

---

65. Barbette Stanley Spaeth, "Epistles: Classical Corner: Paul, Prostitutes, and the Cult of Aphrodite in Corinth," *Biblical Archaeology Review*, 49:1, Spring 2023, https://www.baslibrary.org /biblical-archaeology-review/49/1/35.

way—oneness of id..ntities, oneness of family, oneness of futures, not "God-designed" etc. In other words—marriage. "But we really love each other and are committed to each other," someone might say. Yeah, but apart from a marriage covenant, you know that either of you could walk out whenever and however you want. Where you have no covenant, you have no real commitment.

Physical oneness without soul and life oneness creates a half-human reality. Just like separating the body from the soul produces a zombie, seeking a physical connection with someone while ignoring the soul components creates a zombie-like relationship. (Zombies seem to feature a lot in this book. I didn't start this book intending that. Creepy fellers, those zombies.)

Our culture believes that Christians have too low a view of sex, not appreciating the joy it adds to life. On the contrary, Paul says, Christians have a really *high* view of sex, recognizing that God made it with tremendous power and potential, a beautiful reality to be enjoyed in the right context—between a man and a woman in a marriage.

Sexuality within heterosexual marriage, Paul explained, was a divinely ordained institution that would let us taste the very nature of the Trinity (Ephesians 5:21–32). The consummate union between two beings with biological differences, within a context of lifelong commitment to faithfulness, was meant to be like touching a little part of heaven.

Just Chill Out?

I've been asked before, "Why are you Christians so down on sex? It's not a big deal."

Paul disagreed. His carefulness regarding sex was not because he undervalued it, but because he recognized the power of what God created it for. It is so powerful, he told the Corinthians, that they must flee sexual immorality. It's a sin not just against God or their spouses, he said, but against the very nature of their souls.

Let's consider that more deeply: "Flee from sexual immorality. Every other sin a person commits is outside the body, but the sexually immoral person sins against his own body. Or do you not know that your body is a temple of the Holy Spirit within you, whom you have from God? You are not your own, for you were bought with a price. So glorify God in your body" (1 Corinthians 6:18–20).

First, Paul reasons, if our bodies are the temples of God, where the Holy Spirit dwells, then we take God with us to the prostitute's lair, the porn hub, the adulteress's bedroom. Every Christian should shudder at that thought: *I take him with me everywhere.*

Second, as we've seen, sexual sin is not like most sins. It attacks your own soul. Many say, "But if it's two consenting adults, what's the harm? If they love each other, how is it wrong? And even if it's prostitution, if both are of age and consent, how can it be damaging? And isn't pornography a victimless sin? Someone gets paid to show their body and somebody else gets enjoyment from that." No, Paul says. Extramarital sex produces much destruction, not least of which occurs in a person's own soul.

Years ago, I read a book called *Hooked*, written by two noted board-certified obstetrician/gynecologists. The book, which is not a Christian one, describes the effects of having multiple sexual partners on your brain, especially when you're young. Casual sex actually rewires your brain, they say, in a way that makes genuine, lasting, selfless relationships much more difficult. They say, "The individual who goes from sex partner to sex partner is causing his or her brain to mold and gel so that it eventually begins accepting that sexual pattern as normal. . . . The pattern of changing sex partners therefore seems to damage their ability to bond in a committed relationship."[66]

In his book *Closing the Window: Steps to Living Porn Free*, author Tim Chester adds: "You can no more 'try out' sex than you can 'try out' birth. The very act produces a new reality that cannot be undone."[67]

Outside of God's design, there is truly no "safe sex." To say it bluntly, you cannot protect your soul with a condom.

---

66. Joe S. McIlhaney and Freda McKissic Bush, *Hooked: New Science on How Casual Sex Is Affecting Our Children* (Chicago: Northfield Publishing, 2008), 43.
67. Tim Chester, *Closing the Window: Steps to Living Porn Free* (Downers Grove, IL: InterVarsity, 2010), 123.

God tells us to avoid casual, carefree sex because it causes disease in our souls.

God has wired us so that sex mimics marriage. It creates "marriagelike ties" whether we desire that or not. Tim Keller described it this way in *The Meaning of Marriage*:

> Even if you are not legally married, you may find yourself very quickly feeling marriage-like ties, feeling that the other person has obligations to you. But the other person has no legal, social, or moral responsibility even to call you back in the morning.
>
> This incongruity leads to jealousy and hurt feelings and obsessiveness if two people are having sex but are not married. It makes breaking up vastly harder than it should be. It leads many people to stay trapped in relationships that are not good because of a feeling of having (somehow) connected themselves.[68]

Does this remind you of the plotline of every episode of *Friends* you've ever seen?

Again, Paul is not supporting an anti-sex mindset. Quite the opposite. Sex is good in the right place at the right time with the right person. It's incredibly powerful, one of life's most beautiful mysteries. Sometimes I compare it to fire.

---

68. Tim Keller, *The Meaning of Marriage* (New York: Riverhead, 2011), 260.

Is *fire* good or bad? Well, it depends. Fire is powerful and capable of doing both good and great harm. In my house, I want fire in the right place at the right time—my fireplace. I don't want fire in my basement or the kids' rooms. What is good and beautiful in one context becomes horrific and dangerous in another. (By the way, one of the biggest preaching snafus I ever experienced when I was trying to make the above point, and I meant to say, "Fire in the fireplace is awesome. Fire in your couch is not." But instead, I said, "Sex in the fireplace is awesome!")

One place where the destructive "fire" of our sex-crazed culture burns out of control is in the massive pornography industry. Our city may not have a temple with a thousand prostitutes like Corinth, but we have tens of thousands of pornographic websites accessible 24-7.

Here are the facts:

- Porn traffic on the web every day is more than the online traffic of Amazon, Netflix, and Twitter combined.[69]
- The porn industry in our country takes in more money than Major League Baseball, the NBA, and the NFL combined.[70]

---

69. Aman Jain, "Porn Sites Gets More Visitors Than Netflix, Amazon And Twitter," ValueWalk.com, updated September 18, 2021, https://www.valuewalk.com/porn-sites-gets-more-visitors-than-netflix-amazon-and-twitter/.
70. Lyndon Azcuna, "The Porn Pandemic," LifePlan, October 28, 2021, https://www.lifeplan.org/the-porn-pandemic/.

- One in five searches on mobile phones is for sexually related content.[71]

Many see porn as a victimless crime, a casual release of a physical urge. But here's what is really happening:

- Many of the women in those videos are victims of human trafficking.[72]
- Every woman in those videos is someone's daughter. Imagine the hurt within their own family.
- As the authors of *Hooked* demonstrate, porn rewires the brain in fundamental ways, killing the capacity for lifelong and satisfying relationships because intimacy is viewed as a selfish satisfaction of an urge.
- Porn trains your mind to start looking at the opposite sex as a commodity. The person's body is a selfish tool to use. Often, because of the demeaning and sexist nature of pornographic images and videos, viewers begin to see women (or men) as objects with no soul.

---

71. "Pornography Statistics," Covenant Eyes, accessed August 3, 2023, https://www.covenanteyes.com/pornstats/.
72. "By the Numbers: Is the Porn Industry Connected to Sex Trafficking?", Fight the New Drug, https://fightthenewdrug.org/by-the-numbers -porn-sex-trafficking-connected/ https://theexodusroad.com/porn-and -human-trafficking-the-facts-you-need-to-know/

- Porn trains the mind to think a real body isn't good enough; only one body is good enough, and eventually your spouse's body is not good enough.
- It sets up unrealistic expectations for your spouse's performance in the bedroom. Porn stars are actors.
- People cannot put these experiences and fantasies behind them when they get married. A porn appetite has scarred them.

Porn is not a pastime, like watching soccer or playing Wordle. It dramatically changes who you are. It leads to higher rates of depression, lower rates of sexual satisfaction, and the destruction of countless marriages. Experts now believe that porn is addictive, just like heroin.[73]

But Isn't Sex the Best Part of Life?

Ironically, when it comes to sex, our culture seems to speak out of both sides of its mouth. In one moment, sex is casual and "just physical," no big deal. But in the very next breath, we are told that sexual pleasure is the apex of human happiness. They say if you haven't had sex (or if you aren't having good sex), then your life is woefully incomplete.

Jesus did not agree. In Matthew 19, in his longest sermon on marriage, Jesus spoke about eunuchs. Eunuchs

---

73. Zachary Pottle, "Is Porn Addiction Real," Addiction Center, last updated March 2, 2023, https://www.addictioncenter.com/community/is-porn-addiction-real/.

were people in Jesus's day who, for some reason, could not get married. Some were born with defective genitalia; others were forcibly castrated. Still others, Jesus said, voluntarily chose the life of a eunuch so they could be more useful in the Kingdom of God.

Many in Jesus's day said, "Poor eunuchs. They are missing out on the best part of life." Jesus said, "No way! They get equal participation in the kingdom of heaven."

Romance and sex are signposts pointing to a relationship much greater than themselves—the love of God for us and the intimate connectedness of Christ's body. Missing out on the symbol is no big deal if you get to experience the reality. Speaking of Matthew 12:48–49, John Piper says:

> "[Jesus] came into the world to call out a people for his name from all the families into a new family where single people in Christ [or people not in traditional families] are full-fledged family members on a par with all others, bearing fruit for God and becoming mothers and fathers of the eternal kind. . . . Marriage is temporary and finally gives way to the relationship to which it was pointing all along: Christ and the church—the way a picture is no longer needed when you see face to face."[74]

---

74. John Piper, "Single in Christ: A Name Better than Sons and Daughters," *Desiring God* (blog), April 29, 2007, http://www .desiringgod.org/resource-library/sermons/single-in-christ-a-name -better-than-sons-and-daughters.

Bottom line? It is possible for single people to live full, thriving, and abundant lives, filled with love and happiness. Consider this: every time you pray, you pray to a man who died as a thirty-three-year-old single adult. And he experienced the most joy-filled, purpose-rich life of anyone who ever walked the face of the earth.

God is concerned about your diet of sex. But not because he's trying to kill your fun. Quite the opposite. He knows how unsatisfying and destructive sex can be when we pursue it the wrong way. He knows that the sexual "freedom" our neighbors are pursuing will only ever lead to dead ends and relational emptiness. He has a lot to say about sex *because he invented it*, and his commands aren't strict prohibitions keeping us from the "good stuff"; they are invitations into a free, safe, and flourishing life. God wants the good life for us.

Do you trust him?

Some Good News

I know many people approach the issue of sex with deep regret and pain. You may be thankful that God gives clear rules, but you're also ashamed of how you've broken them— or how others broke them with you in ways that hurt you.

The gospel is that *God does not see you according to your past, sexual or otherwise*. There is no purity in us apart from the blood of Jesus. He sees us as new creations in him. That's why Jesus entered this world—because there's no true purity in any of us. He died so those who believe in him can be identified by their righteousness in him. As 2 Corinthians 5:17 tells us, "Therefore, if anyone is in Christ, he is a new creation. The old has passed away; behold, the new has come."

New. Not broken. Not sinful. Not damaged. But *new.* That's how God sees you. If you have received Jesus, he has cleansed you from your sin and is making you a new creation—a cherished son or daughter in his family.

You don't become his child through sexual purity but through adoption by grace into his family. And that adoption alone gives you the joy, meaning, and identity that empowers you to say no to the urges of immoral sex and to live in the fullness of fellowship with your divine Companion, Brother, Father, and Friend.

Jesus says to you now, "Neither do I condemn you; go, and . . . sin no more" (John 8:11).

12

If I'm a Christian,
Why Do I Keep on Sinning?

In 1886, Robert Louis Stevenson wrote the classic *The Strange Case of Dr. Jekyll and Mr. Hyde*. (My definition of a "classic" book is one everybody has heard about but nobody has read. Usually it sits on a shelf in a richly bound leather cover next to *Moby-Dick*.) But this book might be one worth picking up, because it's a fascinating analysis of the human heart. Stevenson, a believer, was posing a question believers since the apostle Paul have struggled with: Why do I struggle so much to do the right thing?

In the story, Dr. Jekyll, a fine, upstanding citizen, is frustrated because it seems like a bad part of him coexists with the good part—and the bad part is always holding back the good. He calls himself an "incongruous compound" of good and bad.[75]

---

75. Robert Louis Stevenson, "Henry Jekyll's Full Statement of the Case," in *The Strange Case of Dr. Jekyll and Mr. Hyde*, online supplement from Project Gutenberg, 1886, 2008, updated May 22, 2023, https://www.gutenberg.org/files/43/43-h/43-h.htm.

Being a chemist, Dr. Jekyll develops a potion that separates these two parts so that only the good part comes out by day. Unfortunately, the bad part, Mr. Hyde, comes out at night. The name *Hyde* is derived from "hidden" or "hideous." The two have independent reign over the doctor, with neither restraining the other.

To his horror, Dr. Jekyll finds that the evil part of him is far more evil than he had imagined. Mr. Hyde's every thought is centered on himself. He's a spiteful, angry, vengeful murderer.

Dr. Jekyll explains what he has learned through this process, which is "that man is not truly one, but truly two"; he is not technically a hypocrite because both sides of him are completely sincere.[76]

Wow. I know I can identify with that. I feel that "incongruous compound" of completely opposite personas living uncomfortably inside me. When I became a Christian, the intensity of this struggle made me question whether I was a Christian. I believed when I accepted Christ that he had made me a new creation. But if I was a new creation, why did I struggle so much with those old desires?

Had my salvation not "taken"? What was I missing? Was there a booster shot? I wasn't yet inoculated against the basest kind of sinfulness, and it bothered me.

---

76. Stevenson, "Henry Jekyll's Full Statement of the Case," in *The Strange Case of Dr. Jekyll and Mr. Hyde.*

Even though Jesus has declared peace with me, I still find my heart often at war with God. Why is that? Is something wrong with me?

We Still Have the Old Flesh

I find comfort in knowing that the apostle Paul, the greatest missionary and church planter in the Bible, with twelve books in the New Testament credited to him, struggled—just as we all do—with sin. In his letter to the Romans, Paul addressed this Jekyll/Hyde conflict inside himself, writing, "I am of the flesh, sold under sin. For I do not understand my own actions. For I do not do what I want, but I do the very thing I hate. Now if I do what I do not want, I agree with the law, that it is good. So now it is no longer I who do it, but sin that dwells within me" (Romans 7:14–17).

Notice that Paul wrote these verses in the *present* tense. He did not say, "I was a sinner, but then I met Jesus and got better," but rather, "My desires are all out of whack *now*." Paul desired to do righteousness, yet inside him, even as a believer, lurked this Hyde-like, sinful desire at war with himself.

Then he makes this shocking statement: "For I know that nothing good dwells in me, that is, in my flesh. For I have the desire to do what is right, but not the ability to carry it out" (Romans 7:18).

Man, does *that* sound familiar! That sinful nature is, of course, the flesh. *Flesh*, as Paul uses it, means more than just skin and muscle. It encompasses everything you are—mind, body, will, desire—without Jesus. In all of those things, Paul says, there is no good. Nothing. In Romans 3 Paul made it clear that we are sinful cesspools who, apart from God, can't do a lick of good no matter how hard we try. Why? The flesh. The sinful nature. It exists inside us all.

The new me has died to sin, having been resurrected to life by Christ. His Spirit has united itself to my spirit and now forms the center of me. But there's also the old me— the old man, the cranky grumbler who wants this and that, who desires the "bad ol' days" of sin, who prefers slavery in Egypt to the promised land of Jesus.

It's as if I have two fans inside me watching the same game—cheering and jeering at opposite times, both wishing the other one would just die.

Paul goes on in Romans 7 with an insightful rant:

For I know that nothing good dwells in me, that is, in my flesh. For I have the desire to do what is right, but not the ability to carry it out. For I do not do the good I want, but the evil I do not want is what I keep on doing. Now if I do what I do not want, it is no longer I who do it, but sin that dwells within me.

So I find it to be a law that when I want to do right, evil lies close at hand. For I delight in the law of God, in my inner being, but I see in my members another law waging war against the law of my mind and making me captive to the law of sin that dwells in my members. Wretched man that I am! Who will deliver me from this body of death? Thanks be to God through Jesus Christ our Lord! So then, I myself serve the law of God with my mind, but with my flesh I serve the law of sin. (Romans 7:19–25)

Paul's cry is my cry. I want to do good, but I just can't seem to do it well or do it consistently. I always end up making a mess. It's that sin inside me, the other law, that wages war against my new spirit in Jesus. Like Paul, I feel that wretchedness, a deep disgust in myself.

The Battle Rages On

The truth is, the Christian life remains a battle until the day you are fully resurrected as a new person in Jesus. And that is by design, for reasons I'll explain in a minute.

Maturity is learning to apply the finished work of Christ to the unfinished work of sanctification, like sending out like little gospel warriors to bring unruly parts of your body into subjection to Christ.

On November 11, 1918, the world powers agreed to an armistice at 5:10 a.m., ending the brutal fighting of World War I. The cease-fire was to commence at 11:00 a.m. Word spread within an hour, but the fighting did not stop, especially on the Western Front. Even with a cease-fire and the promise of peace, skirmishes broke out and people died.

The same thing happened in World War II as the Allied Forces invaded Berlin. The war was technically over, yet the fighting continued. The settlements of victory had to be applied to the places of struggle.

When I became a Christian, I surrendered to God and he declared peace with me, putting the powers of resurrection in my heart, but I kept the old flesh. These two sides fight inside us all, constantly and unrelentingly.

This is what most people don't understand: when you become a Christian, the old self doesn't just go away, and its craven desires don't weaken. The Holy Spirit doesn't enter your life and kick out the flesh. It now exists with the old self.

You have a choice. You give the Spirit power over the flesh by choosing the Spirit and denying the flesh. Every decision to be obedient to the Spirit weakens Hyde and empowers Jekyll.

The battle starts from the recognition that Jesus has already secured the ultimate victory. That changes your perspective of the fight. Stop choosing the loser (the flesh). You are in Christ, the victor.

If you keep choosing the flesh, you will fall into a spiral of powerlessness. In fact, when you let sin win, its power *multiplies* in you. It comes back stronger. In Galatians 6:7, Paul warns us, "Whatever one sows, that will he also reap." He is talking specifically about how sowing sinful habits into our lives increases their power over us.

It's like the Bermuda grass that my neighbor planted next to our previous home. The thing about Bermuda grass is you can't isolate it into one little section of the yard. Left unchecked, it will take over your whole space. My dad told me that unless I put up some kind of barrier, soon my whole yard would be Bermuda grass too. (I didn't want Bermuda grass, so I just moved.)

If you give occasion to your anger, it will make you an angrier person, not less angry. Venting your anger doesn't reduce its power over you; it increases it. Dwell on lust and you'll become consumed by it, unable to resist its impulses.

You can't be neutral in this war against sin. As the Puritan John Owen said in his book *The Mortification of Sin*, "Be killing sin or it will be killing you."

God Lets Us Struggle with Lesser Sins to Keep Us from the Biggest One

After reading the accounts of tons and tons of great saints describing their battles with sin, I've become convinced (with them) that God lets us struggle with the lesser sins to strengthen us in our fight against the greatest sin: pride. Struggling against sin keeps us humble and tethered to God's grace in gratefulness.

I know that for me, if I walked around easily victorious over sin, it would probably lead me to the conclusion that I'm pretty awesome at this obeying-Jesus thing. And that would, ironically, make me more like Satan, proud in my abilities and glorying in my accomplishments. My righteousness would push me further from God, not closer.

God lets me struggle with the little stuff so I will be even more closely tethered to his grace, and so I will exclaim with Paul:

- "Wretched man that I am! Who will deliver me from this body of death?" (Romans 7:24).
- "Nothing good dwells in me, that is, in my flesh" (Romans 7:18).
- "I have been crucified with Christ. It is no longer I who live, but Christ who lives in me" (Galatians 2:20).

Or, as Jesus reminds us: "Apart from me you can do nothing" (John 15:5).

In my library I have a book of letters written by John Newton, author of the famous hymn "Amazing Grace." One of my favorite letters is one he wrote in his eighties to a friend. In the letter, Newton confessed that he had always assumed that after walking with God for fifty to sixty years, he'd have found complete victory over certain temptations.[77] Yet at that point in his life, some of those temptations felt

---

77. This is a common theme in Newton's letters. Here is one of the more concise quotes capturing the idea: "The unchangeableness of the Lord's love, and the riches of his mercy, are likewise more illustrated by the multiplied pardons he bestows upon his people, than if they needed no forgiveness at all. Hereby the Lord Jesus Christ is more endeared to the soul; all boasting is effectively excluded, and the glory of a full and free salvation is ascribed to him alone." Found in "Advantages from Remaining Sin," in *Letters of John Newton* (Banner of Truth, 1976), p 133. See also his letters titled "Causes, Nature, and Marks of a Decline in Grace," "Believer's Inability on Account of Remaining Sin," and "Contrary Principles in the Believer," within the same volume.

stronger than ever. At first, that thought depressed him, and he wondered if something was fundamentally wrong with him spiritually. Maybe he wasn't even saved.

But he then realized that God let him struggle with sinful temptations, *and probably would until the day he died,* in order to keep him from the worst sin: failing to cherish God's grace. True growth in grace, he said, doesn't mean getting to a place where you feel like you no longer need God's grace, but growing in your awareness of just how desperate you are for it.

God may let you struggle with certain sins to keep you closely tethered to his grace. That doesn't mean you ever stop praying for victory or that he won't ever give it this side of heaven—just that God is up to something good even in delaying his answer to your requests for sanctification.

Honestly, I look at the slate of megapastors who have fallen in ministry and wonder if their success got them to a place where they lost their dependence on God. They weren't inherently worse people than I am. But when one is successful, it is so dangerously easy to think, *I've got this.*

The moment you start trusting in yourself, you start to fall.

Remember: Faith is about resting your weight on the "chair" of Jesus. Begin resting your weight on *anything* else—including your ability to manage this Christian life thing—and you're headed for trouble.

So when I hear that whisper of temptation, I fight it by thanking God for the places he has let me struggle—because there I am (still) learning to lean on God.

You learn to lean on God in failure, not in success. It's like theologian John Stott says, "Pride is your greatest enemy, humility is your greatest friend."[78]

A Practical Way Forward

I hope you don't read the above and think, *Well, I guess there's no hope. I should just go ahead and embrace the mess.* That's not what God wants. Scripture commands us, after all, to fight sin, and it promises us that we can and should make significant progress against it in this life. To that end, it gives us a handful of important instructions for fighting sin. Here are three practical ways you can lean on Jesus in your struggle against sin:

1. Lean into Resurrection Power

In Paul's discussion of his personal struggle against sin, he gives this practical advice: "Likewise you also, reckon yourselves to be dead indeed to sin, but alive to God in Christ Jesus our Lord" (Romans 6:11 NKJV).

Reckon is from a Greek word Paul has used before: *logizomai.* (You might remember that we talked about it in chapter 1 while discussing Romans 4:5.) It means "credited." Paul explained that when we first trusted God's promise to

---

78. John Stott, "Pride, Humility, and God," in *Alive to God*, eds. JI Packer & Loren Wilkinson (Downers Grove, IL: InterVarsity Press, 1992), 119.

remove our sin, God credited our faith as righteousness. The word is an accounting term that means looking at one thing and considering it to be another.

In Romans 4, *God* was doing the reckoning. Well, now, Paul says, it's our turn to do it. We are to reckon (count, credit) ourselves as already dead to sin, even though sin still feels very much alive in us. As we do, God infuses the power of new life into us. Literally, by believing we are in the resurrection, God infuses into us the power of resurrection. Paul is not talking about a mental trick or the power of positive thinking. God really does release resurrection power—the power to live the Christian life—into us as we believe the gospel again and again.

In Christianity, believing is the way to becoming.

Sin's power may feel strong, but we have the assurance that God's ever-stronger power is at work in us.

2. Lean into the Spirit

Paul assures us that we are utterly powerless in our flesh to overcome sin's temptations. But what we are unable to accomplish in our flesh, he says, God supplies in the Spirit. Once more, Galatians 2:20 says: "I have been crucified with Christ. It is no longer I who live, but Christ who lives in me. And the life I now live in the flesh I live by faith in the Son of God, who loved me and gave himself for me."

Christianity is not about us overcoming sin *for God*. It's about God overcoming sin *in us*. Paul said our "hope of glory" was not us for Christ but Christ in us (Colossians 1:27). Paul was saying, "I'm not even the one fighting sin anymore. It's Christ in me."

December 1941 was a dark time for Great Britain. World War II was not going well, and the nation lived with the constant fear of a German invasion. But on the morning of Sunday, December 7, when Germany's ally, Japan, attacked Pearl Harbor, US President Franklin Roosevelt told British Prime Minister Winston Churchill, "We are all in the same boat now."

Churchill later wrote in his memoir, "No American will think it wrong of me if I proclaim to have the United States at our side was to me the greatest joy. . . . England would live; Britain would live. . . . All the rest was merely the proper allocation of overwhelming force. . . . I went to bed and slept the sleep of the saved and thankful."[79]

What transformed Churchill's attitude from one of despair to one of hope? The confidence that "overwhelming force" had just joined his side. Nothing in the war had tangibly changed—Hitler was still on the offensive—but Churchill rested in the assurance of victory that came from the promise of overwhelming force.

The finished work of Christ, the resurrection, and the gift of the Holy Spirit are the "overwhelming forces"

79. Winston S. Churchill, "80th Anniversary of Attack that Brought the United States into the Second World War," International Churchill Society, November 28, 2021, https://winstonchurchill.org /publications/churchill-bulletin/bullertin-162-dec-2021/pearl-harbor.

promised to us in salvation. So, although Paul laments, "What a wretched man I am! Who will rescue me from this body of death?" he can immediately rejoice in the answer: "Thanks be to God through Jesus Christ our Lord!" (Romans 7:24–25 CSB).

Sin is real. But so is the power of God's grace. And even if I can't see it yet, or feel it yet, I know God's power is there. He's never lost a battle. He's never lost one of his own, and I won't be the first. Neither will you. What God started, he will complete (Philippians 1:6). So lean into God's power available in the Spirit.

3. Lean into the Spiritual Disciplines

Finally, a great way to fight sin is to institute ancient spiritual disciplines. Throughout the centuries, saints, mystics, and "ordinary" Christians have found these practices helpful in making progress against the relentless Dr. Hideous. Here are just a few I've found particularly helpful.

Fasting. Fasting has multiple purposes—creating space for prayer, for instance, or standing in solidarity with the poor. But one of the most essential elements of fasting is starving the flesh in order to train the soul to feast on the Spirit. I'll admit: Fasting is my least favorite spiritual discipline. But there is hardly any substitute for the tangible way that fasting makes me lean into God. In fasting, our bodies lead the way in proclaiming our dependence on God, and our souls are weaned away from the satisfaction of physical urges as fulfillment.

Radical accountability. Radical accountability is nearly as uncomfortable as fasting. If you're like me, the idea of opening up every aspect of your life to other people is terrifying. You probably share a little bit with people in your small group, but not *too* much. You keep the confessions socially acceptable and light-hearted. But radical accountability goes further, giving a small number of people nearly complete access to the cavernous dysfunction of your heart. In true accountability relationships, you have permission to ask each other tough and uncomfortable questions about money, relationships, work, motivations, internet history, bitterness, fantasies, and everything in between. It's a bit like my annual physical at the doctor: I don't love it, but it keeps me healthy.

Memorization. Memorization has fallen out of favor in some parts of the evangelical world, and I get the resistance. Given how much work it takes to memorize (and *keep* memorized) a number of Bible verses, this can "feel" like a works-based approach—as if God will automatically bless us based on how many verses we store in our noggins. But nothing else has given me more practical assistance in my fight against sin and growth in godliness. When you hide God's Word in your heart, you give the Spirit the ability to call those words to mind in times of need. God's word is life, the Sword of the Spirit that slays temptation. But the Spirit can't draw a sword you haven't put it in the sheath.

Counter-talking. Counter-talking is a practice I've only recently begun to learn about, even though it has a long history in the church. Essentially, this is a type of prayer in which you identify what idolatries are most active in your heart and mind, then write out in words the shape the idols take in your heart. Then, applying Scripture, you speak directly against those idolatries with the relevant biblical truth. So, for instance, I struggle with the lie that "the good life means an abundance of possessions." As a result, I'm tempted to give only enough to keep myself from feeling guilty—and never in a way that affects my lifestyle or threatens my savings. As an example of counter-talk, I wrote all that down on a card, along with the responses, "Do not lay up for yourselves treasures on earth" and "For one's life does not consist in the abundance of his possessions" (Matthew 6:19; Luke 12:15).

Do these four practices seem too extreme? Many Christians I know seem to believe that semiregular church attendance and occasional Bible reading are enough to fight against the power of sin. But, honestly, that's like trying to use a water gun to put out a house fire. These ancient practices can help drive the Word deep into the heart in a way that transforms us from within and cuts off sin's power at the root. They are radical, yes, and they require commitment; but we must do whatever it takes to subdue sin.

Finally, be encouraged. Remember that being tempted doesn't mean you're losing the war against sin. In fact, it's just the opposite: if the enemy had already won, he wouldn't be fighting you at all. He'd be resting. An enemy increases its attack to make the target weary.

You aren't a helpless and defenseless target. You have an arsenal of defensive weapons and an ally called the Holy Spirit. You have the promise of overwhelming force. And you've got something even Churchill didn't have—the certain knowledge that the war has already, finally, convincingly been won.

When Jesus said, "It is finished," he meant it (John 19:30). And that gives you the strength to go on.

CONCLUSION

The Lie Revisited

And so we arrive at the end—twelve truths that can serve as anchors to your faith. Let's return one more time to the lie so we can put it away forever. It's the lie that will keep you from pressing deeply into these and other questions, which is exactly what God wants you to do: *the fact that you have doubts and difficult questions makes you a bad Christian, or maybe not even a Christian at all.*

It may seem strange to end a book about truth with a lie, but this lie has everything to do with finding the answers discussed in this book.

You see, many people feel they have a problem because they have a question.

When I first verbalized my questions about faith, I did so thinking I would get weird, pitying looks in response. Instead what I got were looks of relief. Those looks seemed to say, "Oh, you've wondered that too?"

News flash: we all have basically the *same* questions. Paul said, "No temptation has overtaken you that is not common to man" (1 Corinthians 10:13). You can apply this to "questions," too, because questions are a kind of temptation. The same basic questions and doubts are familiar to all of us. Some of us are just brave enough to verbalize them. Or brave enough to pick up a book that promises to answer some of them. You were in that group. Good job.

Christianity should be a college of constant learning. One of my favorite descriptions of the Christian life was inspired by the ancient church father St. Augustine and codified 700 years later by Anslem, the Archbishop of Canterbury. The Christian life, he said, is *faith seeking understanding*.[80] Not faith growing out of understanding, or faith that doesn't care about understanding. But faith *seeking* understanding. I feel like that's a pretty good description of my Christian journey: faith seeking understanding. Maybe you feel that way too.

I have several favorite apostles. Thomas might be my most favorite, though, even though he doesn't get the same attention as Peter and Paul. That may be because he didn't write a bunch of books like those attention-hogs did. (Just kidding!) However, he's earned a nickname that has made him a favorite of Christians for two thousand years: *Doubting Thomas*. Thomas had questions and doubts, but

---

80. "What does the motto 'faith seeking understanding' mean?" Got Questions Ministries, updated January 4, 2022, https://www.gotquestions.org/faith-seeking-understanding.html.

thankfully his were not of the soul-destroying kind. He was the kind of person with a foot poised to go either forward or backward with God. Thomas's doubt drove him closer in with Jesus.

In John 11:16, Thomas says to the other disciples, "Let us also go, that we may die with him." Not a lot of doubt there. Later in John 14:5, he responds to Jesus saying, "Lord, we do not know where you are going. How can we know the way?" These words sparked Jesus's famous statement, "I am the way, and the truth, and the life" (verse 6).

Thomas was ready to go and ready to die; he just needed some clarification. When Jesus appeared to the other disciples, Thomas wasn't in the room for some reason (he probably got selected for the Starbucks run). When he returned, Thomas listened to the others' eyewitness account that Jesus was alive and walking through walls. He then responded, "Unless I see in his hands the mark of the nails . . . I will never believe" (John 20:25).

But when Jesus reappeared days later, it was for Thomas. Thomas replied, "My Lord and my God!" (John 20:28). Thomas was the first disciple to make a full and unequivocal acknowledgment of who Jesus actually was: Lord and God. Once Thomas had the answer and proof, he was all-in. In fact, according to the traditions of Syrian Christians, Thomas was the first Christian missionary to carry the gospel to India, where he was martyred.

Now that you've heard answers to some of your questions—or at least learned there are answers out there—what will your response be? Some doubters *like* doubt because it keeps them from committing. Other doubters, like Thomas, use their doubts to go all-in on truth. Which are you?

I hope you continue to ask questions and search for truth. I hope your faith always seeks understanding. As in the case of Thomas, Jesus will bring you the answer in some way, shape, or form. If not now, in heaven. I've made peace with the fact that some questions I probably won't fully know the answers until heaven. Deuteronomy 29:29 says, "The secret things belong to the LORD our God, but the things that are revealed belong to us and to our children forever."

Bad news in that verse: there are "secret things."

More bad news: you may not learn what they are on this side of heaven. They belong to God, not you.

Good news: You have enough "revealed things" to believe and obey until you get there.

Remember, faith is accepting what you cannot understand based on what you can. Whether or not you get the full answers to your questions, commit to the greatest truth ever uttered on earth: Jesus Christ is the Son of God, risen from the dead. When you don't know an answer, you can still know him, confident that he *does* know and that he will answer in time.

And that's no lie.

Just like it's no lie that I placed fourth in the spelling bee and Davy Crockett really is my great, great, great, great uncle.

Sadly, however, I've never shared avocado toast with Nicolas Cage.

Yet.

There's still time.

Mr. Cage, if you read this book, I'd love to hear from you. Email me at requests@jdgreear.com. Come on, Ghost Rider. I don't want to be Left Behind. You're a National Treasure.

ABOUT THE AUTHOR

J.D. Greear is the pastor of The Summit Church, in Raleigh-Durham, North Carolina. Under Pastor J.D.'s leadership, the Summit has grown from a plateaued church of 300 to one of over 12,000. Pastor J.D. has led the Summit in a bold vision to plant one thousand new churches by the year 2050.

Pastor J.D. Greear has authored several books, including *Essential Christianity* (2023), *What Are You Going to Do with Your Life?* (2020), *Searching for Christmas* (2020), *Above All* (2019), *Not God Enough* (2018), *Gaining by Losing* (2015), *Jesus, Continued . . .* (2014), *Stop Asking Jesus into Your Heart* (2013), and *Gospel* (2011). *Summit Life with J.D. Greear* is a daily, half-hour radio broadcast featuring the teaching of Pastor J.D. and cohosts multiple podcasts.

Pastor J.D. completed his Ph.D. in Theology at Southeastern Baptist Theological Seminary. He served as the sixty-second president of the Southern Baptist Convention. Pastor J.D. and his wife, Veronica, are raising four awesome kids: Kharis, Alethia, Ryah, and Adon.

ACKNOWLEDGEMENTS

I have so many people to thank for making *12 Truths and a Lie* a reality, but in particular I want to thank Chad Price and Erik Weir for the vision of getting it started, Dave Schroeder for giving us the opportunity, and the trio of Matt Miglarese, Cliff Johnson, and Dana Leach for making it happen. I also want to thank the entire team at J. D. Greear Ministries for their tireless, selfless, and unrelenting service for the Kingdom. For you all, this is clearly ministry, not employment. Thank you. And to all the volunteers . . . sheesh. I can't even begin to imagine our ministry without your dedicated service in it. You have given not only of your time and money but also of "your very selves" to God's work here.

I also feel an overwhelming debt of gratitude to Chris Pappalardo and Troy Schmidt for their excellent, erudite, and often sharply humorous assistance in the writing of this book. Thank you for the hours and hours of review and brainstorming, as well as the patience to go through these manuscripts again and again to get it right. Clearly, you're working for the Kingdom.

To Matt Love, Spencer Smith, Justin Rand, and especially Daniel Riggs, whose dedication to *Ask Me*

Anything and constant encouragement to keep pressing on, even when we're weary, has kept this all moving forward. Thanks for being Aaron and Hur to me, keeping my hands constantly lifted.

And thanks to the positive, encouraging team at K-LOVE for their willingness to take a chance on this project and their endurance in making it happen! You guys are great. Love your heart for the world and your commitment to take your stewardship responsibilities so seriously. God has blessed you with success, thank you for using it to multiply Kingdom treasure.

To the elders of The Summit Church: thank you for being a faithful leadership team. You have challenged me to engage with ideas like *12 Truths* and enabled me with the bandwidth to make it possible. You make serving at the Summit a true joy and I can't imagine a better band of brothers to be flanked and surrounded by.

And, of course, to my faithful wife of 23 years, Veronica. Thank you for patiently listening to me flesh these ideas out over dinner on "date nights." I couldn't imagine a better life and ministry partner than you. Finally, as always, to my four children—Kharis, Allie, Ryah, and Adon—in everything I've said or written for the past 20 years, you all have been in the back of my mind, often jumping to the forefront of it. Truly, as the apostle John said in 3 John 1:4, I have no greater joy than to know that my children are walking in the truth. I love you all greatly. And I hope that, one day, your children and your children's children will come to know the love of the Heavenly Father as well.

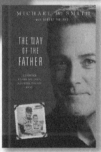

If you loved *12 Truths and a Lie*, receive monthly resources from Pastor J.D. Greear when you become a Gospel Partner.

Gospel Partners are an integral piece of the J.D. Greear Ministries team helping boldly proclaim the gospel through *Summit Life with J.D. Greear* radio, TV, and podcast ministry as well as print resources.

Join us in helping others dive deeper into the love of God through the gospel of Jesus Christ.

learn more
at jdgreear.com or call us at 866.335.5220.

Summit Life
with J.D. Greear

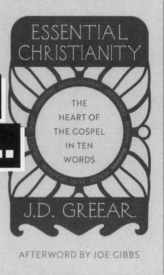
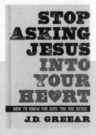